Theodore Roosevelt Among the Humorists

THE HODGES·LECTURES

Theodore Roosevelt Among the Humorists

W. D. Howells, Mark Twain, and Mr. Dooley

BY WILLIAM M. GIBSON

UNIVERSITY OF TENNESSEE PRESS

KNOXVILLE

9/1980

gen. l.

PS
430
G47

Clothbound editions of University of Tennessee Press
books are printed on paper designed for an effective life
of at least 300 years, and binding materials are chosen for
strength and durability.

Library of Congress Cataloging in Publication Data

Gibson, William Merriam, 1912—
    Theodore Roosevelt among the humorists.

    (The Hodges lectures)
    Bibliography: p.
    Includes index.
    1. American wit and humor—History and criticism.
2. Satire, American—History and criticism.
3. Roosevelt, Theodore, Pres. U.S., 1858–1919, in
fiction, drama, poetry, etc. 4. Howells, William
Dean, 1837–1920—Political and social views.
5. Clemens, Samuel Langhorne, 1835–1910—Political
and social views. 6. Dunne, Finley Peter, 1876–1936—
Political and social views. I. Title.
II. Series: Hodges lectures.
PS430.G47   817'.4'09   79–17592
ISBN 0–87049–263–2

CONTENTS

ILLUSTRATIONS

PREFACE

The Hodges Lectures were established in memory of John Cunyus Hodges, who was Professor of English at the University of Tennessee from 1921 until his retirement in 1962 and Head of the Department of English there from 1937 on. As a scholar he was particularly interested in the eighteenth century, especially in the works of William Congreve. As a teacher he was noted for his concern with Freshman English, as evidenced by his popular *Harbrace Handbook*. As a friend of libraries and of colleagues at the University, especially younger ones, he left substantial bequests. The Hodges Lectures are intended to be a tribute to him in all these aspects of his career.

The first series of Hodges Lectures was delivered on October 23, 24, and 25, 1978 by William M. Gibson of the University of Wisconsin on the subject "Theodore Roosevelt among the Humorists." Professor Gibson received his advanced degrees from the University of Chicago, and he taught at Purdue University, the University of Chicago, Williams College, and New York University before going to Wisconsin. He has been a Fulbright lecturer in Italy and a U.S. Educational Foundation lecturer in India. He has held fellowships from the Guggenheim Foundation and the National Endowment for the Humanities and grants from the latter agency and from the American Council of Learned Societies. From 1963 to 1969 he was Director of the Modern Language Association's Center for Editions of American Authors. Professor Gibson is an eminent authority on American Literature of the latter half of the nineteenth century. He has edited letters and works of Howells, Clemens, and James, two of whom are represented in his Hodges Lectures.

Professor Gibson's Hodges Lectures reflect his thorough acquaintance with his subject, his interest in relating literature to history and to general cultural currents, and his wit and urbanity. It is, as he concluded, significant that all three writers whom he considers—Howells, Twain, and Dunne—drew a distinction between the private and the public Roosevelt. All three expressed a genuine liking for the former, but an opposition or at best a satirical attitude toward the latter. All three sharply criticized Roosevelt's imperialistic bent and his fondness for wild game hunting, to a lesser degree his advocacy of large families and the "strenuous life." Dunne's responses were by far the most satiric but most penetrating. All suggest that American writers of whatever period have preserved a deeply humanitarian impulse and a willingness to engage authority, in whatever form, in a contest over the rights of government as opposed to the rights of man.

—NATHALIA WRIGHT
June 1979
University of Tennessee

ACKNOWLEDGMENTS

I wish to thank most cordially first, Nathalia Wright and her colleagues at the University of Tennessee who invited me to give the Hodges Lectures, and then Gordon N. Ray and the John Simon Guggenheim Memorial Foundation, with the members of the Research Committee of the University of Wisconsin at Madison, who provided blessedly free time in which to read and write. Mary E. Bradish and Douglas J. Leonard helped with research and verification responsibly and intelligently. Jane A. Renneberg once again turned crabbedly written manuscript into clear printer's copy. The Houghton Library, Harvard University; the Henry W. and Albert A. Berg Collection of the New York Public Library, Astor, Lenox and Tilden Foundations; and the Howells Edition Center at Indiana University kindly permit me to quote from unpublished manuscripts—mostly letters—of Howells and Mark Twain.

David J. Nordloh, Don L. Cook, and Jerry Herron have aided me in finding and gaining access to the manuscript letters of W.D. Howells at the Howells Center; and W.W. Howells representing The Heirs of W.D. Howells permits me to quote from them. Mr. Nordloh turned up for me the fine caricature of WDH. Similarly, Frederick Anderson, with aid from his assistant in the Mark Twain Papers, Dahlia Armon, before his untimely death most generously let me compound my debt to him; and Thomas G. Chamberlain, President of the Mark Twain Company, has given me leave to quote occasional unpublished passages from Mark Twain's manuscripts. Louis J. Budd advised me concerning a Mark Twain manuscript. Elizabeth Wetherell searched Princeton to no avail for a report of Clemens' blistering attack, made in the Princeton Library in March 1904, on President Roosevelt's policy in Panama and the Philippines. John M. Cooper, historian and colleague here in Madison, voluntarily read my manuscript and helped me look through Theodore Roosevelt's eyes more often than I had. I am very grateful to all these friends and scholars and friends of scholars.

W.M.G.
June 1979

Theodore Roosevelt Among the Humorists

1. TR AND CONTEMPORARY
AMERICAN WRITERS

Democracy in the United States is two hundred years old. From its inception, and far back into colonial life, Americans have been looking to the future for "an America of art and thought," as Henry Adams put it, with great audiences to match its writers. Partial realizations of this dream occurred in the literary renaissance of the 1850s, only a little less intensely perhaps in the 1890s, and again richly in the 1920s. But many if not most nineteenth-century American writers, like Emerson, tended to distrust popular acclaim on the one hand and to seek no part, on the other, in the political power structure, including the electing of the President. Some of them scorned it, or pretended to. Henry Adams is again illuminating. In the fictional character of a distinguished party-giver in Washington named Arthur Bonnycastle, Henry James has Adams say in a story of 1885, "Hang it . . . let us be vulgar and have some fun—let us invite the President."[1]

At the time of the Revolution, the founding fathers were often true men of letters and capable writers, like Franklin, Jefferson, Hamilton, Madison, Paine, Freneau. Later, Washington Irving, James Russell Lowell, and Bret Harte accepted diplomatic posts, it is true. Hawthorne received a lucrative consular job at Liverpool from Franklin Pierce, his friend and college classmate, in return for writing a campaign biography of that most undistinguished President. Mark Twain published Grant's *Memoirs*. It is simply a fact, however, that American men of letters and American Presidents since the Revolution and before Theodore Roosevelt have had little to do with each other, and that these relationships, whatever their extent and character, remain mostly unexplored.

As the nation enters its third century, a few signs of change may be noted. John F. Kennedy asked Robert Frost to read a poem at his inauguration, and Frost responded with "The Gift Outright." President Carter continued Kennedy's gesture by inviting the South Carolina poet James Dickey to read at his inaugural. The creation of the National Foundation on the Arts and the Humanities by Lyndon B. Johnson and the U.S. Congress is certain to have continuing effect in the Republic of Letters.

It is against this background that I wish to trace a kind of composite portrait of a very popular President who called himself "a literary feller," whose taste in literature was conservative and conventional, who read voraciously and at high speed, who wrote voluminously, and who probably entertained more writers at the White House than any President before or after him. Perhaps it is less a composite portrait than it is a triptych of similar though scarcely identical impressions of Theodore Roosevelt created by three writers of the day, W.D. Howells, Samuel L. Clemens ("Mark Twain"), and Finley Peter Dunne ("Mr. Dooley"). I shall focus, perhaps I should say at once, primarily on the images of TR created by the three humorists and only secondarily on Roosevelt's sense of himself in his writings or on his actions as they have been presented by his apologists, like Jacob Riis or Herman Hagedorn. (I have relied for fact more heavily on the biographies of Henry F. Pringle and William Howard Harbaugh than on any others.) Howells and Mark Twain were more than twenty years older than TR, Dunne a decade younger. Why these three?

One basic reason is simply that Howells and Mark Twain and "Mr. Dooley" were the best humorists in America during the years of Roosevelt's power in the presidency—the scarcely known Dunne is only now I believe beginning to come into his own. All three were satirists of great skill and force, and all three took a strong interest in the politics of the gilded age, the turn of the century, and the progressive era. Dunne became much sought after by TR, flatteringly enough, yet kept his commentator's independence. Mark Twain tended to like Roosevelt the man but to despise the politician and expansionist. Howells, who had written campaign biographies of Lincoln and of Rutherford B. Hayes, followed Roosevelt's career with a divided mind, like Clemens. But all were fascinated by TR's fabulous energy and attracted by his friendliness to letters, and all of them commented extensively, in public and in private, on TR the skillful politician.

2

The three best satirists of the age also shared the same background and long experience in journalism and had become practiced commentators and editorialists, often behind the loosely fitting masks of such pseudonyms as "the higher journalist" and Mark Twain and "Mr. Dooley." Despite a rather wide spectrum of reactions to TR, they read each other's writings upon publication, and when Clemens discovered that he needed a really select audience for his verbal efforts to "vex mankind," he asked Howells and Dunne to join him in the "God-damned Human Race Luncheon Club." In short, if I may anticipate my conclusion in this study of literature and politics, Howells, Clemens, and Dunne come very close, in my judgment, to a just and lasting delineation of their many-sided subject. This is by reason of their fascination with Roosevelt, their frequent personal encounters with him over the years, their Mugwump detachment as satirists in and out of the game of politics, their sensibility to character, their rather special awareness of constitutional principles and the American past, and their fluctuating, sometimes despairing, sometimes hopeful, imagination of the American future. The writings of the three humorists on TR will thus serve as evidence for an exercise in biography and politics and history. The writings will also be considered as rhetoric, as writing designed to persuade—that skill which every good satirist has mastered. An art that has been a million times debauched, it remains a high art still, essential to the endless dialogue between writers searching and sifting for the truth.

I shall deal with Howells' impressions of Roosevelt in the second chapter, Mark Twain and Dunne's in the third and fourth. Before turning to Howells, however, it may be well to note the reaction of certain other representative American writers of Roosevelt's day—especially of E.A. Robinson, Henry James, Stephen Crane, Edith Wharton—to suggest what strong mixed feelings he aroused in the literary community.

E.A. Robinson dedicated *The Town Down the River* to TR in 1910 and closed his volume with a poem about Roosevelt called "The Revealer." Robinson, in fact, believed correctly that he owed his poetic life to the President; in 1904 he wrote Kermit Roosevelt, "your astonishing father . . . fished me out of hell by the hair of the head." That is to say, the President, after he had read and reviewed favorably Robinson's *The Children of the Night*, had gotten the poet

3

out of the New York subway tunnel excavation into the Customs House. It is rather surprising that Roosevelt should have liked Robinson's small town dramas of madness and suicide—but he enjoyed the "sad mysticism" and the music of the poems even when he did not fully understand them, he said.[3] George Ade, Indiana humorist and playwright, strongly supported TR in nearly all of his policies, and the shy Joel Chandler Harris was devoted to Roosevelt, in part because the Roosevelt children were brought up on the Uncle Remus stories. John Hay was of course secretary of state to both McKinley and Roosevelt, and was deeply involved in the plans and negotiations for the Panama Canal, that splendid engineering feat and questionable political venture. Hay was also a man of letters who found TR almost equally amusing and impressive and who wrote a sonnet of tribute "To Theodore Roosevelt" on Christmas Eve, 1902, called the "Fruitful Years of Fame."[4] But the President, however delightful and epigrammatic he had found Hay, after Hay's death pronounced him a "figure-head." Hay's intimacy with Henry James and Henry Adams he thought "impaired his usefulness as a public man" because he admired and emulated their "tone of satirical cynicism." As for Adams, he purely distrusted Roosevelt's coming to power and wielding it with "abnormal energy," though when TR left the White House in 1909, he said to him, "I shall miss you very much."[5]

As for Henry James, one can scarcely imagine a greater contrast in temperament and taste than that between the novelist and the Rough Rider. On reading a James story in the Yellow Book (1894) Roosevelt protested, "What a miserable little snob Henry James is. His polished, pointless, uninteresting stories about the upper social classes of England make one blush to think that he was once an American."[6] Ten years later, James the literary master felt flattered to dine at the White House and found "Theodore Rex" a "really extraordinary creature." But at heart, James considered TR "a dangerous and ominous jingo" and "the mere monstrous embodiment of unprecedented and resounding noise."[7] Conversely, John Burroughs and John Muir, both companions of Roosevelt on trips into the Western wilderness, were drawn to him by his passion for conservation and his real naturalist's knowledge and both wrote books about their experiences.

Teddy and the Big Stick. The New York *Globe*.

Stephen Crane's opinions of Roosevelt, which were mixed, arose from his coming to know TR well first as police commissioner in New York City and then as commanding officer of the Rough Riders in Cuba. In this first phase, Crane grew intensely critical of the New York City police, especially after he was pilloried in the papers for quixotically defending a chorus girl charged by one Becker with soliciting. Later, Roosevelt the President clashed with one of Crane's friends, asserting that Crane was a man of bad character who consorted with loose women, while the friend hotly defended Crane as a champion of young women persecuted by the police. In the Cuban period, Crane was less intent on praising the Rough Riders and their colonel than he was on crediting the U.S. Army regulars with no less courage but with greater competence in battle. Nonetheless he wrote that Roosevelt worked "like a cider press" for his troopers, buying rations for them with his own and borrowed money and putting hard pressure on the Quartermaster Corps for quinine. "Let him be a politician if he likes," Crane said: "He was a gentleman down there."[8] Thus it happened that Roosevelt praised Richard Harding Davis at length in his *Rough Riders*, but mentions Crane only as a realistic modern novelist who mistakenly attributes "complicated emotions" to fighting men, who in real combat in Cuba "behaved quite simply."[9]

Edgar Lee Masters, who achieved popular success with the *Spoon River Anthology* in 1915, was invited by Colonel Roosevelt to talk over the poems. After a day with TR, he represented their talk in a dramatic poem, "At Sagamore Hill."[10] They had discussed Celtic poetry, bass fishing, free verse, lion hunting, wildflowers, history, and American wars, but TR wanted particularly to know why Masters scorned "our Philippine adventure" and the soldiers who served with him and with Frederick Funston. He sent Masters a copy of his autobiography after the visit, and asked him to read the chapter on Panama.[11] In their talk, Masters must have defended his taking sides with John P. Altgeld against what he would call in his own autobiography, *Across Spoon River*, the "puerile imperialism of McKinley and Roosevelt."[12] Masters had openly attacked Roosevelt in *The New Star Chamber* in 1904, particularly for a Chicago speech in 1900 excoriating license and disorder, presumably among the Democrats. But Masters' poem is not merely a defense of his own views; it

6

depicts a man of great cordiality and charm—even a degree of humility. His tone is thus very different from that of H.L. Mencken, who publicly damned TR in "Roosevelt: An Autopsy,"[13] for his philosphical kinship with Kaiser Wilhelm, and who wrote Dreiser the day after Roosevelt's death, "the man was a liar, a braggart, a bully and a fraud, but let us not speak evil of the dead."[14]

Ellen Glasgow took much the same view of Roosevelt as Masters. Prepared to dislike him for his big game hunting, in 1914 she met the colonel for the first time and surrendered, she says, not to his "dubious literary insight" but to his "human magnetism." Only being born a Roosevelt, she surmised, prevented him from becoming a great human being as well as a great leader.[15] No such compunction troubled Edith Wharton, who had known TR since youth and who was a distant cousin of his second wife. Although they met infrequently, they met as old New Yorkers with many friends in common. The President liked her novel *The Valley of Decision* and her familiarity with Lewis Carroll, she remembered. Whether receiving an honorary degree at Williams College or attending a reception after giving a lecture at the Sorbonne, Roosevelt delayed ceremonies and flouted protocol to talk with whom he pleased, she reported, his intellectual curiosity being "almost as fervent as his moral ardours."[16] She felt Roosevelt to be her friend and suffered acute sorrow at his death. Her chief tribute to him was a poem "Within the Tide," which I find the most moving of the poems inspired early and late by Theodore Roosevelt. A "slow-circling, brooding, sixty-line blank-verse" elegy, it gains form from a legend that Wharton had read about in *The Golden Bough* to the effect that when a man dies "his dead friends come at twilight to the shore and escort him by boat to the lands of the blessed."[17] Never before, as Wharton conceives the event, did such a "freight of friends," so vast a throng, appear on the Long Island beach in the dusk. Givers, strivers, men that "loved right more than ease, / And honor above honors," in Wharton's elegy they lead Roosevelt to the towering ships and take him out on the ebb tide "on some farther quest."[18]

Robinson, Henry James, Stephen Crane, Edith Wharton, John Hay, Henry Adams, John Burroughs, John Muir, Edgar Lee Masters, H.L. Mencken, Ellen Glasgow, Thorstein Veblen, Willa Cather, Robert Frost—one might add still others to fill in an entire spectrum of feeling and judgment about Theodore Roosevelt. None of these writers, however, were Roosevelt watchers to quite the degree or in quite the sense as W.D. Howells, Mark Twain, and F.P. Dunne. What then of Howells and Roosevelt?

2. TR AND W.D. HOWELLS:
"I am faint thinking of him"

From the 1890s, soon after Howells and Roosevelt first met, to the war-filled turn of the century and Roosevelt's sudden accession to the presidency following the assassination of William McKinley, the relation of the two men grew from their common literary concerns. Howells reviewed several of TR's books, shared an interest with him in the vulgar life of New York City, and during his brief editorship of *The Cosmopolitan* commissioned articles from TR for that journal.

His first review, of Roosevelt's hurriedly-written biography, *Gouverneur Morris*,[1] published in *Harper's Magazine* for July 1888, called the book a "brilliant sketch," for Roosevelt had fully understood what a patriot-aristocrat Morris had been, a man possessing "distinction," in Matthew Arnold's sense of the word. Benjamin Franklin was the antitype to Morris, Franklin conversely sharing the "common humanity" of most great Americans. So that Morris was, Howells concludes, a "brilliant finial, but the temple of our liberties in no wise rests upon him." This distrust of "distinction," this respect for common humanity, Howells first acquired from his own upbringing and his admiration for A. Lincoln, as his campaign biography shows. It was given even greater depth in middle life, at this time, from his reading of Tolstoy. Howells believed in short that we Americans, "above all other peoples on earth . . . are of the ancient and noble lineage of Antaeus . . . potent with feet on the ground, lifted weak as a column of falling water."[2]

A year later in 1889 Howells found Roosevelt's *The Winning of the West*[3] sharply analytic in distinguishing between English and French character and policy in the trans-Allegheny west, and to an "uncommon and delightful degree anecdotal." The author as well "does full justice to the courage and sagacity of the Indians," Howells observed. His one reservation concerns TR's "rather peculiar liking

9

for the Scotch-Irish Presbyterians, "those bleak Calvinists," his "peculiar misliking" for the Quakers, and his open dislike of the Moravians. This sect in Ohio had Christianized the Indians very successfully, only to see their "inoffensive converts" massacred by American frontiersmen. TR had written, "No greater wrong can ever be done than to put a good man at the mercy of a bad man, while telling him not to defend himself or his fellows." Howells comments: "Another moralist, however, in whom the Moravians seem to have trusted, said: 'Resist not evil: but whosoever shall smite thee on thy right cheek, turn to him the other also. . . . Love your enemies, bless them that curse you, do good to them that hate you.' " In the abstract, Howells concludes, "we will not venture to decide between these authorities"; but in particular, his own past research on the Moravian settlement of Gnadenhutten showed that war would not have availed the converts.

A year later, in the fall of 1890, Roosevelt wrote to Howells to say how pleased he had been by Howells' comment in the "Editor's Study" of *Harper's* on the political aspects of Harold Frederic's novel, *Seth's Brother's Wife*, "politics being rather my hobby."[4] These aspects are "curiously true to life," TR insists—except for the political boss turning "semimugwump" on the last page of the book. "I always draw a breath of relief when I read . . . of the real motives and methods of the politician," TR added; for "Our average educated man is singularly ignorant" of politics.[5]

Howells responded to Roosevelt's final query in the letter, as to when they might meet again to talk literature, that he would like to see him, questions or no questions. His life-long awareness of the ways and tricks of politicians, in the country, had been once illumined by something John Hay had told him, "so I was able to recognize the truth of Frederic's picture when I saw it."[6] In the same year as this exchange about Harold Frederic and New York state politics in his fiction, Roosevelt told Howells that he and Mrs. Roosevelt had read Howells' *A Boy's Town* once through and then had gone back to re-read favorite parts. "The feelings of the boy in many cases I could thoroughly understand for the excellent reason that I have felt them myself," he wrote.[7]

In the spring of 1892, Howells accepted an offer from John Brisben Walker, a millionaire socialist, to edit a new journal, *The*

Cosmopolitan. Howells hoped to make the monthly both a popular success and a means of elevating public taste. It was with both ends in mind that he secured contributions from Sarah Orne Jewett and Henry James and from Frank R. Stockton, Stephen Crane, and Theodore Roosevelt, whose reputation as civil service commissioner in Washington, D.C. continued to grow. Knowing TR's intense feeling about American writers and the American past, Howells commissioned Roosevelt to write two essays for the *Cosmopolitan*. The first, "A Colonial Survival," vigorously denied Rudyard Kipling's recent charge that New York City was unsafe, and took Agnes Repplier to task for asserting that the American Civil War produced no poetry. "Colonialism gone crazy," he called her article.[8] The second, a review of "Francis Parkman's Histories," was a particularly shrewd assignment because Roosevelt's *The Winning of the West* had been dedicated to the Brahmin historian. But Walker and Howells soon found themselves disagreeing on subjects and assignments for the magazine. As Roosevelt wrote a friend, "The hitch comes in with Walker, who has deprived Howells of control . . . My Parkman article, two months after Howells, having asked for it, had accepted it with thanks, was returned by Walker, on the ground that the subject was not one in which his readers took any interest."[9] Roosevelt published the Parkman review in *The Independent*, and Howells soon resigned the editorship.

The relation of the two men was by now cordial. In December 1892, Roosevelt wrote to enlist Howells' aid in the political campaign of his close friend Cabot Lodge for senator in Massachusetts. Would Howells write the editor of the *Boston Transcript* asking him to support Lodge? And would he have lunch with him?[10] But at the same time he was asking for political favor, TR was objecting that Howells, like Hamlin Garland, was suffering from "morbidity" in his literary pieces and was taking what he called "a jaundiced view of life." This was not an uncommon development, he added, of the reform spirit, unfortunately.[11] A few years later, Roosevelt told Arlo Bates, concerning Bates's recent volume of literary criticism: "It did me good to see the straightforward fashion in which you dealt with Maeterlinck, Ibsen, Verlaine, Tolstoi and the decadents . . . . I wish Howells could be persuaded to read and profit by what you have written."[12] Just what TR meant by morbid, jaundiced, and decadent

11

as they apply to Howells' writing is not wholly clear—*The Shadow of a Dream* (1890), which is a study of marital jealousy, might be so regarded—but is seems much more likely that Roosevelt is referring to Howells' Christian socialism and his passion for Tolstoy, not to speak of Garland's enthusiasm for Henry George and the single tax. There is a good chance, too, that Roosevelt means that Howells had a penchant for mixed or unhappy endings in his novels, and that he, Roosevelt, detested realism even at the mildest.

Nonetheless, friendly relations persisted. In the fall of 1897 Brander Matthews had a luncheon in New York city for TR, who was about to resign as police commissioner after a most active but largely unsuccessful two years of attempted police reform. In Garland's report, Owen Wister and Howells and Roosevelt made the occasion "illustrious," Roosevelt overflowing with stories of police experiences and of "my cops," he called them. Howells repeatedly asked Roosevelt to tell them further stories of foreign peoples and street ceremonies in New York City. "You must put these impressions into writing before they are overlaid by your Washington experiences" as assistant secretary of the navy, Howells said, "they have great value as history." When TR replied that he had no time to write, Howells countered: "We will be content with a record such as you have given us today." Talk to a stenographer, Howells urged: "Get it down in essentials and refine it afterwards."[13] In the end Roosevelt never did write up his rich experience as a police commissioner, and it was undoubtedly a loss. But Howells himself pioneered in much New York City street history, and his articles and novels, especially *A Hazard of New Fortunes,* encouraged other slum writers whom Roosevelt took to lunch and read and talked to: Jacob Riis, Lincoln Steffens, Stephen Crane, and Abraham Cahn. Cahn's *Yekl* Howells must have sent to TR earlier in the year. Roosevelt wrote back, "That was a very remarkable study of the life of the East-side Jew; I enjoyed it much."[14]

In short, during the first decade of their acquaintance, Howells and Theodore Roosevelt shared a good many interests and activities having to do with literature and reform and the Bowery of New York City. But the sinking of the American battleship *Maine* in Havana harbor early in 1898 and the war with Spain in Cuba which ensued signaled a new era of armed conflicts. Roosevelt and Howells now parted company on two crucial issues: warfare and the size of American families. Roosevelt precipitated the second of these divergences in a presidential address in February 1903. For years he had been preaching that the cardinal national sin was "wilful sterility in marriage"—having no children or only one or two—or as he called it "race suicide."[15] Conversely, he had many times over praised large families, virile men, and womanly women. Now, in the February speech, he called anyone who hesitated to have children "a criminal against the race . . . the object of contemptuous abhorrence by healthy people."[16] Howells at age sixty-six answered the President at age forty-four in an entire essay, which he called "A Personal Question." It was a debate between the Family Man and the Higher Journalist, one of Howells' familiar masks.[17]

The Family Man opens the debate by asserting that this is not a civic question or a social question but a personal question—that "we are not here to perpetuate races or nationalities, but to save our souls alive. . . ." Quoting TR again, the Family Man does not deny that the greatest joy springs from the "bringing up of many healthy children." But what, he inquires, if the children are sickly, and a father must walk the floor with a sick child? What of the recurrent bills for rent, coal, groceries, meat, gas, clothes? If you have leisure and nurses, the Family Man says, go ahead; but if you are middle or lower middle class, "well, wait."

The President talks openly and candidly to his fellow Americans, and that is good, says his critic, but "I wish," he adds, "he would measure his words . . . and measure his thoughts, too." Does the President favor legislation to support the large family when the breadwinner is laid off? Clearly he cannot associate himself with Napoleon, who spoke of children in big families as *chair à canon*—cannon's meat. The American ideal was once a large family; now it may well be, argues the Family Man, that parents are anxious to "secure the future for their children before they launch them into the present," Providence not being always or wholly trustworthy. In fact, says Howells dropping his mask, "I prefer to clear my mind of cant, and I am at the point of chucking the superstition that the children you cannot take care of will be mystically looked after by the moral government of the universe." And besides, says the Family Man as he goes out, the choice belongs to the woman primarily, whether she be a society leader or some average American wife. Whereupon the Higher Journalist finds himself inspired to write a column on the "cowardly behavior of Adam" in trying to make Eve take the responsibility in "that affair of the apple." The tone of Howells' response to Roosevelt is mostly easy enough, but as he had concluded a year or two earlier, "The small family has apparently come to stay." Apparently, too, Howells must have heard from readers of *Harper's Weekly* who favored the President's view. A month later, the Higher Journalist concluded his column, "Oh, *I* am not in favor of race suicide!"

The tenor of Howells' response to Roosevelt was, I have suggested, mostly good-humored and reasonable. But at one point he breaks into cutting irony: the large family is "an old American ideal, like taxation based on representation, and government by consent of the governed, and brotherly equality, and some other things that seem to have gone by the board."[18] Howells is referring of course to the status of Filipinos, bought (as he says elsewhere) at two dollars a head.

The Philippine phase of the Spanish-American war accompanied a wave of imperialist warfare involving many of the world powers, Great Britain fighting the Boer republics in South Africa and the chief European powers putting down the Boxer rebellion in China. That phase also marks an extreme divergence between Roosevelt's intense nationalism and his belief in military virtues, and Howells' internationalism and his Christian pacifism. Howells was distrustful of the war against Spain in Cuba from the beginning. As he had written to Mark Twain in August of 1898, "our war for humanity" was being turned by the McKinley administration into a "war for coaling stations" for the U.S. navy. By October he wrote to Clemens from New York City:

> There is the worst kind of political campaign going on, here, with no hope against Tammany, except Roosevelt, a good, strong, clean man, but a man who did more than any other to bring on the war, and now wants us to have a big army and navy, and go in for imperialism.[19]

Just how divided he was in his mind about TR appears in a letter of November, in which he admits that he is a good deal puzzled how to vote for the governorship of New York State: "I don't want Tammany to come in, and yet I hate to vote for a war man like Roosevelt." He might, he thought, vote the citizens ticket, with such men as Carl Schurz.[20]

In the next few years, Howells' repugnance to colonial warfare grew and manifested itself in a constant rather low-keyed stream of comment—a stream that Mark Twain, finally home from a long stay in Europe, contributed to spectacularly, as we shall see. By the spring of 1902 Howells had two regular channels for literary and social comment, the "Editor's Easy Chair" of *Harper's Monthly Magazine* and a column in *Harper's Weekly*, both unsigned but manifestly his. He had, moreover, freedom to write as he pleased in the *Weekly* from George Harvey, current head of the house of Harper, and the result (he told C.E. Norton) was that he had fairly given the magazine "an anti-imperialistic tone."[21]

In April 1901, for example, he praised a novel by the Filipino José Rizal, "a little saffron man" with a literary gift beyond "our roaring successes," and in May he argued that the men and women who had known war at first hand, in 1861 to 1865, would never have undertaken the Spanish-American war, "whose Dead Sea fruit is still turning to ashes on our lips." They rejected the "superstition that war makes for manliness," but they could not save the current generation from the Spanish War. Contrary to our illusions of patience, justice, and mercy, Howells concludes, we are a "truculent and sanguinary race," with the danger of murderous delirium "always imminent." Proof? A mob burning a Negro at the stake, lately, in Kansas, with no trial and no injury ever proved.[22]

Just how deep the differences between TR and Howells began to run is manifest in Roosevelt's angry reaction to the assassination of President McKinley by an anarchist, Cszogolz. In September 1901, the new President told a close friend that "Hearst and Altgeld, and to an only less degree, Tolstoi and the feeble apostles of Tolstoi, like . . . William Dean Howells, who united in petitions for the pardon of anarchists, have a heavy share in the burden of responsibility for crimes of this kind."[23] TR was remembering the Haymarket Riots in Chicago fifteen years earlier, and Howells' public declaration that the Chicago anarchists had been convicted for their political opinions, not for murder as charged. At the time, in 1886, Roosevelt had told his sister that he and his ranch hands in the Bad Lands would like

15

nothing better than to face with rifles the Chicago mobs even if they were "ten times our number."[24]

Howells' views of the war policy of McKinley, pursued unchanged by Roosevelt, were as jaundiced as Roosevelt's were ebullient and sanguine. In January of 1902 he mustered up all his experience and editorial coolness in an attempt to define the "new Americanism" and its proponent Theodore Roosevelt, the new American. The small war with Spain and the death of McKinley have ended an epoch, he says, and "left the particles of our political substance irrevocably reassorted." The danger coming out of "the Cuban cumber and the Philippine folly" is that the country may settle into the mold of empire, with "wealth-worship" turning into "rank-worship" under a constitution that cannot be stretched to cover that empire. As for Theodore Roosevelt, Howells calls him "a democrat *de facto*," though he is inalienably "an aristocrat *de jure*," and therefore representative of the great current change from the "gentle man" to the "common man." Roosevelt is "perhaps more conspicuously human than any other man who has filled his place." One may fear "his weakness, which is his rashness," says Howells, but one may also trust his strength. Although he may do a rash thing, "he will not do a wrong thing if he knows it." And in sum he is capable of the ambition of being "the best servant this people has ever had."[25] (No evidence I know of exists to indicate that Roosevelt read this particular "Easy Chair," but it is likely he did, for he read and published in the magazines very widely. It would be fascinating to know what he thought of it.)

Howells maintained his critical stance until about 1904 and Roosevelt's election to the presidency. Thereafter, it may be presumed "pacification" in the Philippines, however slow, and Roosevelt's unobtrusive change in the direction of Howells' socialism (a word TR abhorred) led finally to a state of armed truce and of good feeling between them.

In the spring of 1902, Howells took to task, and severely, the Reverend Dr. Bagnell, who was reported as saying, "I would rather have the United States become an empire, with Theodore Roosevelt, or some man like him, as Emperor and have the laws enforced than have this land become a republic of lawlessness and license." The minister was referring to the Sunday closing liquor law in New York

City, which Roosevelt as a police commissioner had once tried to enforce—with only temporary success. Howells reacted strongly. He observed that under such a pure despotism as he favored, the Reverend Dr. Bagnell might himself wind up fighting in the Philippines. He closed his attack by demanding that Bagnell make "an explicit apology to Mr. Roosevelt for mentioning his name in connection with even an imaginary empire," for "that is an offence which, to a true American, savors of insult."[26]

By June of 1902, like other anti-imperialists, Howells was protesting army policy in the Philippines—a policy which at its worst permitted torture of Filipino insurgents by the "water-cure" so called, and included a "scorched-earth" practice, making a "howling wilderness" of Samar, as one general promised. Herod's policy in Bethlehem might be weighed delicately against the actions of American generals in Samar, Howells insisted, [27] and, he lauded "the Presidential position that the tortures used by our troops in the Philippines are of the same moral quality as those inflicted by our citizens in burning negroes within our constitutional limits.[28] In July, a pious correspondent in Colorado suggested that the terrible volcanic eruption on the island of Martinique gave proof of God's omnipotence, and a minor poet named T. Janvier boasted that American troops had "smashed" the Spaniard "by God's decree."[29] Howells observed: "we cannot be too diffident, too delicate, too modest, in our claim to confidential relations with the Almighty . . . ." A little later, taking a Phi Beta Kappa poem by N.S. Shaler as his text, Howells argued that men learn no virtues in war, that peace has its own heroes, and that "it is not rough-riding up San Juan hills alone that is the event of heroism."[30]

Then in September 1904, Howells found a cherished opportunity, as he sometimes did, in reviewing, to arrive at a kind of summing up or overview of current Anglo-American relations. The immediate occasion for this particular "Editor's Easy Chair" was his evaluation of two powerfully contrasting books: Sir George Trevelyan's *History of the American Revolution* and Archibald Colquhoun's *Greater America*. After a satirical glance at international marriages between American plutocracy and British aristocracy, Howells observes:

> At the end of the Spanish war we found ourselves embarrassed with the task of destroying an infant republic in the Philippines, and almost at

the same moment Great Britain had laid upon her the duty of destroy-
ing an adolescent republic in South Africa. Of the two, ours was the
more odious office . . .

the reason of course being that the U.S. had "always professed a
tenderness for republics."[31]

If then, international marriages or a preferential tariff or an uneasy
kinship in imperial ventures will not suffice, what shall the means be
of a true Anglo-American alliance? Literature, Howells replies, not
surprisingly, and specifically history, by such a large-minded and
large-spirited Englishman as Trevelyan. His book, Howells says,
brilliantly portrays the American worthies of the revolution and is
perhaps unique in showing how it was "almost first among good
wars" in the benefits it conferred upon the losers—how English
freedom triumphed. But if Trevelyan's book ought to be "epitomized
for use in schools," Colquhoun's book, flattering and readable as it
is, ought *not* to be so employed. Colquhoun congratulates Americans upon the "coolness with which we have practically ignored our
inherited ideals in our colonial empire," Howells observes. Thus,
"the rights of man are not for man when he is brown, or when he is
yellow, or even when he is pale olive; representation goes with
taxation only when the skin is absolutely white."[32] The author of
Greater America has no doubt about expansion. He speaks of those
who criticize the government policy in the Philippines as "demagogues, cranks, and fanatics," meaning, Howells adds, "such
demagogues as Professor William James, such cranks as Mr. Schurz
or Mr. Schurman, such fanatics as Mark Twain."[33] English and
American imperialists will be drawn together, Howells concludes, by
Colquhoun: other sorts of Englishmen and Americans by such a
history as Trevelyan's, and by the revolutionary ideals it sets forth.
Earlier, in May of 1902, Howells had called the "dream of universal
Anglo-Saxon empire" a "cheap and vulgar hallucination," which
even if it were realized, would end in a "world-wide provin-
cialism."[34] Although President Roosevelt is not mentioned in the
"Easy Chair," the views of Colquhoun on expansion and even the
epithets Colquhoun uses for critics of expansion represent pretty
clearly the Rooseveltian position.

By the time the war developed between Russia and Japan in
February 1904 and came to an end in November 1905 through the

good offices of President Roosevelt, Howells presumably found TR's conciliation praiseworthy. The evidence is slight. Such as it is, in it Howells expresses sympathy "for the common soldiers on both sides, who have no more real interest in the war than we have," and even more for the wives and children of the soldiers, the widowed and orphaned.[35] As for Americans' generally favoring the Japanese, and his own apparent favoring the Russians, Howells confesses, "The truth is I am a Korean sympathizer, and have been from the beginning of the war. . . . I have the single wish that Korea may emerge from the dispute a free and independent Korean republic, perhaps of the type which we are going, a hundred years hence, to set up for the Filipinos."[36] It is characteristic that Howells should keep an eye on over-run Korea when the spotlight was on Russia and Japan.

In the late summer of 1904, before the presidential election, Howells, in England, wrote home to ask what they thought of Roosevelt's chances. "It looks from this distance," he said, "as if Parker might win. When I think of the Republican rascality about the Philippines I could wish them beaten; but I shudder when I think what became of the wretched negroes in the South, under Democratic success."[37] Then a year later, in the early fall of 1905, Howells wrote his sister Aurelia that the President was sympathetic to the idea of appointing their brother Joe to a consular position.[38] He wrote to Secretary Elihu Root at once and told his brother to be as definite as possible in asking for a position in British America or in the West Indies.[39] On October 1, he gave his sister the good news of Joe's appointment to the consulship at Turk's Island in the Bahamas; and on 2 October the President wrote "My dear Mr. Howells" that it had been a trivial act which he was almost ashamed to have Howells thank him for.[40] Roosevelt may have considered his act "trivial," but Howells and his elderly ailing brother did not find it so and the matter was concluded with typical Rooseveltian dispatch.

The following spring, Howells wrote his brother to note the "great stand" Roosevelt had taken in favor of an income tax and inheritance taxes, to check the accumulations of great fortunes." "It is a most daring act," he averred, "but will unquestionably add to his enormous popularity." The press will be down on him, but he could now sweep the country in being re-elected. Roosevelt "is a strange man," Howells said to Joe, "and nobody has yet plucked out the heart of his mystery."[41]

Perhaps the most cordial letter Howells ever wrote to Roosevelt followed, in August 1906, when he congratulated the President for his support of Andrew Carnegie's simplified spelling reform. Such action a hundred years earlier, Howells claimed, would by this time have resulted in a "spelling which would not perpetually confound the reason and insult the intelligence of every child learning to read and write." Howells equally wanted to thank TR for the measures he had urged to restrain the overwhelming accumulation of wealth. And then Howells concluded with comment on the people and with an anecdote, this way:

> I think it is the sense that you are always watchfully with them in what truly concerns them, and that you will not be afraid to show it, which endears you to the people, and even to those who have sometimes been doubters among them, like myself. May I tell you something which I thought pretty at the time, without now seeming to flatter you? I was in the smoking room of a westward Pullman, and an average American who had been all our average variety of citizen, was talking politics, or rather politicians. "Well," I said, presently, "What about Roosevelt?" He turned on me vividly: "Just love him, just *love* him!"[42]

I think it likely that Howells approached the heart of Roosevelt's private charm and public popularity in this tribute. In response, TR explained that he wanted to restrain great fortunes (though not by "violent revolution") and to control corporations, and to enact a good, stiff progressive inheritance tax and a good stiff progressive income tax nationally. Above all "I feel I have laid the foundations for right action," said the President. And he ended by expressing his appreciation most of all perhaps for the concluding anecdote, and by signing the letter "with great regard."[43] That Howells, like Andrew Carnegie and Roosevelt, was serious about spelling reform, as most of his fellow Americans were not, is attested to in an "Easy Chair" of the same period, a witty, fervent, frontal attack on "our impudently false orthography . . . our dictionary spelling."[44] For children having to learn to spell unreasonably, it is a "sin against light and knowledge." It is, says Howells, "an offence to reason, a cruelty to infancy, an affliction to maturity, and a burden to senility."[45]

One activity on which Howells and Roosevelt continued to disagree was hunting. TR of course agreed with Chaucer's monk, who

> yaf nat of that text a pulled hen
> That seith that hunters beth nat hooly men

whereas Howells—who had hunted as a boy in Ohio—believed that hunting belonged to the childhood of the race. "The other night I met at dinner that fine old John Burroughs whom I congratulated on his going out to Yellowstone to hold bears for the President to kill; but he seemed to think it not an altogether enviable office, but to have his latent misgivings"—so Howells told C.E. Norton in 1903. Howells had not then seen a picture of King Edward with a long double line of pheasants he had shot. Otherwise, he said to Norton, he could have told Burroughs that "bears were nobler game, and our prince was by so much in advance of the English boy."[46] Several years later Howells pursued the subject editorially, taking off from a book by a British woman on the pleasures of the hunt. Sport, he maintains, has now become "the gory Dagon of idolatry," and this superstition "has infected the whole civilized world until now the man who hunts . . . is the supreme type of manliness." "We have sent an ex-President into the wilds of Africa to perform its savage rites, he said, and he has come away celebrating the involuntary co-operation of the victims." Comparing TR with the English king and his recent bag, Howells notes that the greater bulk of Roosevelt's bag, of lions and elephants and other big game, is not especially a source for American pride. In fact, "in a strenuous age like ours," he cannot believe that the " 'prolongation of infancy' into permanent boyhood by sport tells much for humanity." Then, speaking his mind, he confesses that he finds British shooting "grotesque and revolting."[47]

Whatever their differences, the taste for literature held in common by Howells and Roosevelt brought them together. Howells found the President's style lively in his messages; he was delighted that Roosevelt thought Brand Whitlock's *The Thirteenth District* "the best political novel written in America"; and he told Madison Cawein that he counted praise from the President valuable "because it is that of a man who lives and feels poetry."[48] The President even told Howells in December 1906 that he read everything Howells wrote as it came out, and asked him to bring E.C. Stedman to the White House for dinner. Although neither writer could make the journey, Howells felt the President's intention was truly kind, and was "very like that very much of a Man."[49]

Some slight contretemps may have arisen from an anonymous interviewer reporting in the *Boston Herald* in June 1907 that Howells' choice for the next President was Charles Evans Hughes rather than Taft, whom TR supported as his successor. Howells wrote to Norton privately that the interview was full of vulgar misrepresentations; and he denied that he wanted Hughes to succeed Roosevelt in a letter to the *New York Sun* later in the month.[50]

Howells' last notable reaction to Colonel Roosevelt, as the President was called after leaving the presidency, is appropriately admiring but mixed. Henry B. Fuller had written to tell his mentor and backer that he had no great liking for his Chicago environment, and no great zest for life as it is lived. Howells responded: "Shall I own such a thing? Not after sitting at breakfast yesterday beside T. Roosevelt, and witnessing the wonder of his zest for everything. He is so strenuous that I am faint thinking of him. No man over forty has the force to meet him without nervous prostration."[51] Humorous exaggeration and all, this is recognizably the man whom Henry Adams called more than abnormally energetic—a man of "pure act."[52]

Howells wished to be scrupulously just in regard to Roosevelt. This is evidenced in his organization of a memorial meeting in honor of Mark Twain, in November 1910, under the auspices of the American Academy of Arts and Letters: as he had told Clara Clemens Gabrilowitsch (and she had agreed), if Roosevelt spoke, it would be a Roosevelt meeting, not a Mark Twain memorial. He would overslaugh President Taft, who should be first, and every other speaker. But Howells thought above all that Clemens' feelings should be respected. He disliked Roosevelt intensely, and at a large dinner he had spoken of Roosevelt with withering contempt. To have Roosevelt praise him would not be fair to Roosevelt himself—he says it reluctantly—for Roosevelt "once granted a favor I asked of him with eager generosity, and I would not seem to forget it." (The favor of course was the consular position for brother Joe.)[53] Happily, diplomacy—presumably Howells' diplomacy—prevailed in the end, and *neither* President Taft nor Colonel Roosevelt spoke at the memorial meeting to Mark Twain.[54] How Mark Twain came to hold Roosevelt in "withering contempt" is the subject of the chapter that follows.

3. TR AND MARK TWAIN
"He is the 'Tom Sawyer' of American politics"

Although in 1906 Mark Twain remarked that he had known Theodore Roosevelt "for certainly twenty years," dining in his company on occasion and enjoying Roosevelt's heartiness and gusto,[1] it was not until his return from several years of round-the-world lecturing, in the fall of 1900, that Clemens began to take a strong, lasting interest in the Vice President soon to become President. That the foremost humorist of the country should begin to follow closely the career of the President of the country is not surprising. Both men over the years had formed intense moral commitments, Clemens' often unconventional, Roosevelt's largely traditional. Thus Mark Twain, fresh from Europe in October 1900, informed a New York audience that he was maintaining strict vigilance in order to "regulate the moral and political situation on this planet."[2] Similarly, as Owen Wister once told Mrs. Roosevelt, TR was at heart, profoundly, a "preacher militant."[3]

But in nearly every other respect the humorist of sixty-six and the President of forty-three were almost contrapuntally different and opposed. To name only a few of the most striking differences. Roosevelt believed in and lived the "strenuous life." Mark Twain insisted that he had never taken any exercise, except sleeping and resting, and that he never intended to take any. "Exercise," he said, "is loathsome."[4] A part of the Strenuous Life, as TR led it, was his passion for hunting, particularly big game hunting in the West of the United States and in South America and Africa, for sport, for food, for museum collections. Mark Twain, on the other hand, hated cruelty to animals and the killing of animals and wrote *A Horse's Tale* and *A Dog's Tale* to protest bullfighting and vivisection. The depth of his hatred may be measured by the image of the town loafers at Bricksville in *Huckleberry Finn*, who amuse themselves by pouring kerosene on a stray dog and touching a match to it.

Reading the newspaper stories of how the President killed a bear in Louisiana, in the fall of 1907, Mark Twain entertained himself and Isabel Lyon, his secretary, with his own burlesque version of the hunt. Really, he insists, it was a cow that was Roosevelt's victim, who in her flight "acted just as a cow would have done . . . with a President of the United States and a squadron of bellowing dogs chasing after her." When the cow's strength was exhausted, according to the humorist, she stopped in an open spot and tearfully said to the President, "Have pity, sir, and spare me. I am alone, you are many . . . have pity, sir—there is no heroism in killing an exhausted cow." But Roosevelt, who is "still only fourteen years old after living half a century," shot the bear in an "extremely sportsmanlike manner" and hugged his guides jubilantly after the kill. He is, Mark Twain then declared, "the most formidable disaster that has befallen the country since the Civil War."[5]

Roosevelt's taste in literature was for the romantic and the epic, and embodied reverence for "the great men and great deeds and great thoughts of a bygone time,"[6] whereas Clemens tended to love the real and especially the "irreverent" or the iconoclastic. Roosevelt's manner of speech and writing was straightforward and simple, while Clemens' was ironic.

A more complex difference, recorded in Mark Twain's autobiographical dictation, arose from the Morris episode in January 1906. A Mrs. Minor Morris had called on the President at the White House to plead the case of her husband, who had been dismissed from military service. A private secretary to the President, one Barnes, had summoned the police and had had Mrs. Morris physically ejected and taken to a local police station. From the episode Mark Twain concludes that Roosevelt, "one of the most impulsive men in existence" wrongly permits himself "impulsive secretaries." Roosevelt, he declares, is "so hearty, so straightforward, outspoken, and, for the moment, so absolutely sincere" that one finds him thoroughly likable, as a private citizen. But these traits make him a "sufficiently queer President."[7] TR is yet "the most popular human being in the United States."[8] The reasons for his great popularity? If the twelve apostles were to come to the White House (Clemens claims) the President would invite them in and say how much he admired their progress. "Then, if Satan should come, he would slap him on the

25

shoulder and say, 'Why, Satan, how *do* you do? I am so glad to meet you. I've read all your books and enjoyed every one of them.' " Anybody—says Mark Twain—could be popular with a gift like that.[9]

Only a few months later, Mark Twain's view of Roosevelt's character had darkened. Offended by TR's "scream of delight" when General Leonard Wood's men killed 600 Moros in the Philippines—men, women, and children—Clemens spoke privately of the President as "fearfully hard and coarse"; "the worst President we have ever had"; yet also "the most admired."[10]

By 1907 Clemens was even more consistently "down on" the President, coming to regard him as a master at self-advertising. He notes the newly made charge that TR had bought the election of 1904 in the final week with money from E.H. Harriman and Standard Oil. He observes that the President is sending Secretary Taft around the world and the U.S. Navy to San Francisco, for advertisement. And he accuses Roosevelt of half-wrecking the industries of the country and reducing the value of all property therein in the Depression of 1907.[11] In short, Mark Twain charges:

> Mr. Roosevelt is the Tom Sawyer of the political world of the twentieth century; always showing off; always hunting a chance to show off; in his frenzied imagination the Great Republic is a vast Barnum circus with him for a clown and the whole world for audience; he would go to Halifax for half a chance to show off, and he would go to hell for a whole one.[12]

It needs to be added that the creator of Tom Sawyer was never exactly averse to the limelight, himself, and that the extravagance of his analysis of President Roosevelt's character is partly due to his dictating an autobiography that was not to be published until long after his death.

Roosevelt, the truly omnivorous reader, began to read Mark Twain early in his life. He also read him widely, taking special pleasure in *Tom Sawyer* and *Huckleberry Finn*—which he included in his own Pigskin Library as "classics"—and in *Life on the Mississippi*.[13] TR did *not*, however, like *A Connecticut Yankee in King Arthur's Court*. He considered Mark Twain a "real genius" but wholly without cultivation or real historical knowledge, who in the book belittled the great knights of the round table.[14] Nonetheless, in

HUCK FINN

June 1904, he sent a special directive permitting Clemens and his family immediate passage through customs when they returned from Italy with the body of his wife Olivia Clemens.[15] TR also paid a rambling, rather vague tribute in a letter to Clemens for his seventieth birthday celebration[16] on 5 December 1905; and he eulogized him after his death as "not only a great humorist, but a great philosopher [whose] writings form one of the assets in America's contribution to the world of achievement, of which we have a right as a nation to be genuinely proud."[17]

One area in which Mark Twain and the President came together—on a small island in a sea of disagreement—was spelling reform. The Simplified Spelling Board was initiated by Andrew Carnegie; Brander Matthews chaired the group; Mark Twain was a prominent member; President Roosevelt endorsed it. At an Associated Press banquet in New York City in September 1906—the same month in which Howells wrote an "Easy Chair" column praising the effort—Mark Twain argued that if the Associated Press were only to adopt simplified spelling for three months, the infallible result would be victory for the forces of reason. After such an experiment, he asserted, "the present clumsy and ragged forms will be grotesque to the eye and revolting to the soul. And we shall be rid of phthisis and phthisic and pneumonia, and pneumatics, and diphtheria, and pterodactyl, and all those other insane words which no man addicted to the simple Christian life can try to spell and not lose some of the bloom of his piety in the demoralizing attempt."[18]

In this same fall of 1906, Clemens poked fun at Roosevelt's strenuous endorsement of large families. The occasion was his speech in the company of Howells and others backing a new copyright law before a congressional hearing in Washington. "Why," he said, "if a man who is not even mad, but only strenuous—strenuous about race suicide— should come to me and try to get me to use my large political and ecclesiastical influence to get a bill passed by Congress limiting families to twenty-two children by one mother, I should try to calm him down. I should reason with him. I should say to him, 'That is the very parallel to the copyright limitation by statute. . . . Leave it alone and it will take care of itself.' " President Roosevelt is not named in the passage—but he is patently the momentary target of Mark Twain's absurd reversal of the Rooseveltian view.[19]

The source of the most fundamental disagreement between Mark Twain and Theodore Roosevelt was the 'imperialist" or "expansionist" policy of McKinley, which TR pursued and broadened throughout his presidency. The men differed on the Boxer rebellion in China and the role of American missionaries there, on the Cuban conflict and especially the war in the Philippines that ensued, on the policy of the English in the Boer War in South Africa, on Roosevelt's "taking" of the Panama Canal, and even on his achieving peace by arbitration between Russia and Japan.

At the beginning of 1901, Mark Twain's wrath against Kaiser Wilhelm, the European powers in China, and the American missionary William S. Ament boiled over in an article called "To the Person Sitting in Darkness," one of the most powerful pieces of invective that Clemens ever wrote. Clemens even declared in an interview that he was a Boxer, and favored the Boxer policy of driving foreigners out of China. In July, Vice President Roosevelt wrote privately to a friend, "The trouble with China was, as with most great questions, that the problem was infinitely complicated; whereas all our prize idiots from Mark Twain and Godkin down airily announced that both the problem and the solution were absolutely simple."[20] Then, in October, at the Yale Bicentennial for a degree, with Mark Twain, President Roosevelt may well have let Clemens overhear him exclaim to a missionary back from Peiping, "When I hear what Mark Twain and others have said in criticism of the missionaries, I feel like skinning them alive!"[21]

This rather ferocious animus in the President against Mark Twain and other anti-imperialists was in fact symptomatic. In a rising storm of popular abuse, the charge soon appeared that Mark Twain was a traitor for opposing administration policy in the Philippines. The measure of Clemens' hurt, resentment, and anger on being branded traitorous becomes clear when one considers the number and weight of the counterattacks he made, published and unpublished, throughout the last decade of his life upon Roosevelt and much of Roosevelt's "Big Stick" foreign policy.

In the first two years of the century, however, Clemens tended to condemn the McKinley administration rather than Vice President Roosevelt for certain dangerous tendencies in American life, as he viewed them. At a Lotos Club dinner in New York City in November

1900, Mark Twain spoke of the Vice President wittily: "We have," he said, "tried an illustrious rough rider for Governor and liked him so well that we made him Vice-President"—in order to "give a little needed distinction to the office." Now, for a while anyway, Clemens continued, "we shall not be stammering and embarrassed when a stranger asks us, 'What is the name of the Vice-President?' This one is known; this one is pretty well known, pretty widely known, and in some places favorably. I am a little afraid," the speaker added, "that these fulsome compliments may be misunderstood . . . . I am not used to this complimentary business; but—well, my old affectionate admiration for Governor Roosevelt has probably betrayed me into the complimentary excess; but I know him, and you know him; and if you give him rope enough . . . ." Mark Twain wound up his joshing by claiming he would have been a Rough Rider and gone to war himself—if he could have taken an automobile rather than a horse.[22]

It was this satirical stance assumed by Mark Twain in regard to the new expansionism and Roosevelt's sudden popularity as a war hero that led the *New York Nation* in the same month, November 1900, to praise the humorist as a commentator on public affairs. Mr. Clemens, said the *Nation* editorially, with his "fatal eye for folly and humbug" has seen the new delusion of grandeur in the United States for the "vulgar hypocrisy it is." He has "even refused to fall down and worship Roosevelt" and has "actually made fun of that solemn man!"[23] Mark Twain remains a "homely and vigorous republican," the editorial concluded, "let who will trick themselves out in the gauds and paste jewels of imperialism."[24]

At another dinner, early in January 1901, Mark Twain explained that he had not voted for either Bryan or McKinley because Bryan was wrong on the money question and McKinley was wrong in sending "our bright boys" out to the Philippines "to fight . . . under a polluted flag."[25] Only a few weeks later at a dinner for Governor Odell of New York, with Theodore Roosevelt on the toast list, Clemens noted that a minister, unnamed, had recently called him a traitor for not fighting in the Philippines. But declared the humorist, when the life of the nation is not in danger, then the nation may be politically divided, "half patriots and half traitors, and no man can tell which from which."[26]

Just how differently Mark Twain and Roosevelt faced the future in

America, at this juncture, Howells disclosed in his report of a friend's analysis of the current American dilemma. The friend—unnamed —was surely Clemens. Howells said:

> He is not himself one of the fatly satisfied Americans who fancy the fulfilment of our mission to mankind in our present welter of wealth and corpulent expansion. Rather he finds that . . . we stand gasping in a tide of glory and affluence that may soon or late close over the old America forever. He speaks darkly of a dying republic, and of a nascent monarchy or oligarchy.

This same friend, Howells concluded, thought it a good thing to create a hall of fame, where the names of Washington, Franklin, Jefferson, and Lincoln set on high might long challenge the eyes of the people.[27]

Just before Christmas of 1901 Mark Twain, on an impulse presumably, wrote to Roosevelt, claiming that he spoke not as a stranger but for the whole nation, saying, "Not Duncan himself was clearer in his great office."[28] Mark Twain presumably means that Roosevelt had done well to retain intact McKinley's cabinet and to maintain McKinley's domestic policies so faithfully. Roosevelt answered from the White House, "Praise from Sir Hubert, my dear Doctor," returning Mark Twain's compliment and alluding to Clemens' recent honorary degree from Yale. The President thanked Clemens heartily for the Christmas greeting, which "touched and pleased" him,[29] and he said, "Approbation from Sir Hubert Stanley is praise indeed."[30]

Before Roosevelt became President, at the death of McKinley on 14 September 1901, Mark Twain had unloosed a truly fearful barrage of criticism against the McKinley administration and the European imperialist powers. Of these blasts at Foreign Secretary Chamberlain of England; President McKinley; General Frederick Funston of the United States Army; the American missionary in China, William S. Ament; the czar of all the Russias; and King Leopold of Belgium, two will have to represent Clemens' furious long-burning wrath. The first, "A Salutation-Speech from the 19th Century to the 20th, Taken down in Shorthand by Mark Twain," appeared in the *New York Herald* on 30 December 1900. It takes the form of a toast and reads as follows:

I bring you the stately matron named Christendom, returning bedraggled, besmirched & dishonored from pirate-raids in Kiao-Chou, Manchuria, South Africa & the Philippines, with her soul full of meanness, her pocket full of boodle, & her mouth full of pious hypocrisies. Give her soap & a towel, but hide the looking-glass.[31]

This carefully wrought, highly effective bit of rhetoric carries a considerable shock in cartooning the United States and other Christian nations as a drunken matron returning from a bout of debauchery, sexual and alcoholic. Clemens tried with considerable success to repeat and expand the attack in a piece which he called "The Stupendous Procession," portraying the same aggressive warring nations led by the twentieth century, "a fair young creature, drunk and disorderly . . . ."[32] But he would not, and probably could not, publish it. The American army general, Frederick Funston, for example, marches in the procession as the Siamese twin of Judas Escariot.[33]

The second representative piece, like its predecessors "To the Person Sitting in Darkness" and "To My Missionary Critics," appeared in the *North American Review* but unlike them failed to hit its target dead center. By now Mark Twain's conviction that human beings were inherently limited and had no freedom of choice was so strong that he must admit it even in his ironic "A Defense of General Funston." The weight of the attack on Frederick Funston is nevertheless heavy. This American general had captured the Filipino leader Aguinaldo by what William James called "a bunco-steering trick"—by methods, that is, which Funston himself admitted were nothing to be proud of. Mark Twain "defends" Funston by asserting that to bribe a courier, to disguise one's self, to accept a courteous welcome, and even to assassinate the welcomers—all are justified by the customs of war. But to accept food when they were nearly helpless with hunger, as General Funston and four other officers did, and then to lift one's hand and weapons against one's host violates all customs pagan and civilized. It is, says Mark Twain, a uniquely base act.

Clemens had written his "Defense" by mid-April, but found it necessary to add a postscript on the fourteenth on a closely related matter, in which he declared:

The President is speaking up, this morning, just as this goes to the printer, and there is no uncertain sound about the note. It is the speech and spirit of a President of a people, not of a party, and we all like it, Traitors and all. I think I may speak for the other traitors, for I am sure they feel as I do about it. I will explain that we get our title from the Funstonian Patriots—free of charge . . . . they are born . . . flatterers, these boys.[34]

President Roosevelt had ordered a thorough investigation of charges of cruelty committed by the American army and its Macabebe scouts against captured Filipino insurgents, and of the torture known as the water-cure. According to the *New York Evening Post*, the President had declared he would personally be answerable for punishing any officers found guilty with the "hardest penalty the law allows."[35]

This is probably the last time Mark Twain praised Roosevelt for any feature of his foreign policy. Certainly by the early fall of 1904, when he wrote "A Brief Biography of the Government" for George Harvey and *Harper's Weekly*, he was becoming persuaded that Roosevelt and the rich were creating a federal oligarchy. He was especially incensed at President Roosevelt's securing land for the Panama Canal "by methods which might have wrung a shudder out of the seasoned McKinley."[36] Mark Twain wrote:

> The Government of the United States was born in the State of New York forty-six years ago, of an old and eminent Dutch family. In the common school, the academy and the university he acquired his civil education; he acquired his military education in the Rocky Mountains in conflicts with the bear; among the cowboys he got his training in the cautious arts of statesmanship and in the delicate etiquette of diplomacy.
>
> In time he became Police Commissioner of New York City, and was a good one. Later he was Governor of his State, under Mr. Platt. After a while he was made Assistant Secretary of the Navy and chief promoter of a war with Spain. Then he resigned and went to his war, and took San Juan Hill, without concealment, but in the most public manner. Nothing in history resembles this engagement . . . .
>
> Next he accepted the Vice-Presidency of the Republican Party, which is the United States. Presently he became President and Government by the visitation of God. By and by he took fourteen million dollars out of the public till and gave it away, dividing it among all elderly voters who had had relatives in the Civil War [a reference to Roosevelt's Executive Order 78, which extended pensions and benefits, in exchange for votes, according to TR's critics]. . . .
>
> When the Government of the United States wanted some territory for a canal, he took it away from the proprietor by the strong hand. The

proprietor was not big and strong, like Russia or England or Germany, and in other ways was not entitled to respect.

When Russian imperial pirates take his merchant ships away from him he tries to be patient. And succeeds.

When Russia violates his mail-bags on the high seas he tries to forget about it. And succeeds.

Still—among us—what he wants he takes. It will be best for us again to elect him Government of the United States on the eighth of November next. Otherwise he will take it anyhow.[37]

The tone of Mark Twain's "biography" is jocular, but the undertone is deeply ironic, and he finally withheld the letter from publication even under the protective signature, "Constant Reader." Curiously enough, according to Harvey's biographer, when such "excellent fooling" came to Roosevelt's attention, "he hugely enjoyed it, and at this very time he accounted both Mark Twain and George Harvey his dear friends."[38] Harvey was now in fact as much opposed to TR as Clemens.

By the time TR was elected in 1904, Clemens had come to a clearer understanding of his attitude toward the President. Just before the election, he begged his old friend, Joe Twichell, a minister, to get out of the "sewer of party politics," where McKinley and John Hay and Roosevelt had led him—soiled public men who were, Clemens insisted, "in private life spotless in character."[39] Even more lucidly in a letter to Twichell a few months later, Mark Twain defined his mixed feelings about the President: "For twenty years I have loved Roosevelt the man and hated Roosevelt the statesman and politician." For twenty-five years, he confesses, a "wave of welcome" has streaked through him in shaking hands with the man. But the politician, vote hungry per order 78 and "ready to kick the Constitution into the back yard," he found utterly destitute of morals and not respect-worthy.[40]

Perhaps the point of greatest revulsion in Mark Twain's view of the President came in 1906 when General Leonard Wood and 540 American soldiers killed 600 Moro guerilla fighters, including women and children, who had fortified themselves in the bowl of an extinct volcano, near Jolo. As Mark Twain recorded the event in his Autobiographical Dictation for 12 March 1906, Wood and his men had climbed the steep slope with artillery; their order had been to "Kill or capture the six hundred"; after a day and a half "battle," fifteen Americans lost their lives—but the six hundred Moros were all dead.

Mark Twain quotes figures of the killed and wounded in the Civil War, and at Waterloo, and in the "pathetic comedy" of the Cuban War—where 1 percent of the American forces had been killed or wounded, and 2 percent of the Spaniards. But in this Philippine encounter, "we abolished them utterly"—Mark Twain says, "leaving not even a baby to cry for its dead mother." He calls it "incomparably the greatest victory that was ever achieved by the Christian soldiers of the United States."[41] The day following the cabled news from the Philippines, President Roosevelt had cabled in return, "Wood, Manila—I congratulate you and the officers and men of your command upon the brilliant feat of arms wherein you and they so well upheld the honor of the American flag." Clemens charges that Roosevelt *knew* the soldiers dishonored the flag. He adds two days later that George Harvey believed the episode might destroy the Republican party and President Roosevelt, but that "prophecies of good things rarely come true." He ends by comparing Roosevelt's joy in this victory with President McKinley's "earlier presidential ecstasy" in "motions resembling a dance" on learning the news that Funston had captured Aguinaldo.[42]

This account of the death of six hundred Moros is unrestrainedly indignant partly perhaps because Mark Twain did not intend it for publication until long after his death. But in a speech prepared for delivery in mid-October 1907, on the occasion of a visit to the United States by the Right Reverend Winnington-Ingram, lord bishop of London, Mark Twain may have declared openly what he dictated to a secretary privately for his autobiography. His theme was "our great country," satirically treated, and he adopted the device of addressing the lord bishop directly, thus:

> Our form of government, sir, is . . . monarchy . . . like your own at home. . . . Yours is hereditary monarchy under a permanent political party. . . .
> You will read and hear much of the President of the United States. Dear sir, do not be deceived—there is no such person. And no such office. There is a President of the Republican party, but there has been only one President of the United States since the country lost Mr. Lincoln forty-two years ago. . . . The party, only, is hereditary now, but the headship of it will be hereditary by and by, in a single family.

Pray do not overlook our patriotism, sir. There is more of it here than exists in any other country. It is all lodged in the Republican party. The party will tell you so. All others are traitors, and are long ago used to the name. . . . We are nearly ripe for a throne, here; in fact all we lack is the name.[43]

One not familiar with the thought of Mark Twain late in his life might suspect him of mere joking in his talk of a coming monarchy under Theodore Roosevelt. But he had predicted a coming monarchy in the United States thirty-five years before[44]—so he recalls in the Autobiographical Dictation of 16 July 1908—and he gives his reasons. Man wishes by his nature to look up to God or to King. Great republics have never lasted. Vast power incites public favorites to dangerous ambitions. The immediate startling proof of his contention is that Roosevelt has named his own successor in the presidency, William Howard Taft.[45] Only a few months later, Mark Twain with something less than perfect logic and consistency admitted that he was going to vote for Mr. Taft, and that "The monarchy is here to stay."[46]

Mark Twain's final word on Theodore Roosevelt, dictated to a stenographer two days after the President left office, gives thanks that the country is rid of Roosevelt the heavy burden, the incubus—though not probably forever. After four years a hostile providence may re-impose "this showy charlatan" whom our people have adored "as perhaps no impostor of his breed has been adored since the Golden Calf." The nation, Clemens predicts, will want him back after he is through with his hunting other wild animals heroically in Africa.[47] Mark Twain died in 1910 and did not live to witness Colonel Roosevelt's effort to be re-elected on the Bull Moose platform, but one may safely guess he would have continued to oppose him in his public character.

As for Mark Twain's fear that Roosevelt might become monarch or dictator of the United States, at our distance in time the fear seems to have been groundless. In the extremely bitter contest between Roosevelt and Taft in the campaign in 1912, however, it was rumored that Roosevelt had gone mad, and that if he could seize the presidency, he would make it an hereditary office. The *Louisville Courier* could see only one issue—in Roosevelt's name and person—"life tenure in the executive office."[48] Charles H. Dana compared TR to the Roman consul Tiberius Gracchus.[49] Thus, Mark Twain's distrust of Roosevelt's ambition may have been groundless—but it was shared.

In the political struggles and wars of the turn of the century, none interested Mark Twain more than the conflict between czarist Russia and imperial Japan. As "The Czar's Soliloquy" published in March 1905, demonstrates, Clemens hoped for the overthrow of the czar in the defeat of the Russian forces by Japan, whereas President Roosevelt shrewdly brought the two powers together at Portsmouth, New Hampshire, and persuaded them to sign a treaty of peace. Roosevelt's intent was to maintain a balance of power in Asia and the Pacific; his reward was the Nobel Peace Prize. But the peace treaty profoundly disappointed Mark Twain. Shortly before it was signed he wrote the editor of the *Boston Globe* that Russia was "on the high road to emancipation from an insane and intolerable slavery," that it was a "holy war" with a high mission, and that that mission was now defeated. Russia's chains were re-riveted, he feared, this time to stay. One more battle would have "abolished the chains of billions of unborn Russians," but now the czar will "resume his medieval barbarisms." "I hope I am mistaken," he concluded, "yet in all sincerity I believe that this peace is entitled to rank as the most conspicuous disaster in political history."[50] The letter to the *Globe* is all the more arresting because it strikes the single negative note in two full pages of letters approving Roosevelt's role in achieving peace. Six months later, Clemens recalled saying to an elderly Russian revolutionary, Tchaykoffsky, "when our windy and flamboyant President conceived the idea, a year ago, of advertising himself to the world as the new Angel of Peace [between Russia and Japan] . . . no one in all this nation except Doctor Seaman and myself uttered a public protest against this folly of follies." He had believed at the time that Roosevelt had "given the Russian revolution its death-blow," and he was of that opinion yet.

Mark Twain differed more often than not, vigorously, with Theodore Roosevelt on turn of the century wars and U.S. foreign policy. What Roosevelt's position was in regard to the cruel exploitation of native labor in the Congo by King Leopold of Belgium has only recently been explored. He may well have agreed with Mark Twain, privately, that the Belgian king's agents in the Congo were ruthless butchers; but for a time he accepted the views of his secretary of state—first John Hay and then Elihu Root—that any formal protest or the creation of a board of inquiry on Belgian policy would constitute interference in the domestic affairs of a friendly nation.

Mark Twain himself reluctantly came to this same view, but not until several months after he had published *King Leopold's Soliloquy*, in September 1905. This was a harsh, often brilliant, condemnation in pamphlet form of Leopold's treatment of workers in the Belgian Congo, with photographs of mutilated Congolese. The work was published by the Congo Reform Association in England and the United States. Clemens' name appeared in it as first vice president of the protest group, and he contributed all financial returns from it to the Association.

A partial solution to the question of Roosevelt's reaction lies in Mark Twain's letter to Mrs. Roosevelt of 27 November 1905. In it, thanking her for her recent "charming hospitality" in the White House, he confesses that he was troubled during the visit because he feared the President did not know that he had "come to Washington to ask for a private word on a public matter." His "citizen-conscience" had in fact forced him to unload the burden onto the President's shoulders. Then after making an elaborate joke about his hardened conscience, Mark Twain again speaks of "appeals which are not made in a personal & sordid interest but in behalf of a matter clothed in the dignity of an honorable & national importance." And he closes, most sincerely, thanking the President for remembering him "when the irremediable disaster of my life fell upon me"—a reference of course to the intervention of TR with the customs people fifteen months earlier when Clemens had returned from Italy with the body of his wife.[52]

Nothing concerned Mark Twain more on 28 November 1905—not even his seventieth birthday, two days away—than the need to expose and to stop King Leopold's atrocities. Hence I conclude that the matter of "national importance" which Citizen Clemens raised with Theodore Roosevelt was a request that the President act openly to condemn Leopold. The same day Clemens wrote a note to Robert Bacon in the State Department,[53] sending him "those Congo documents" and explaining the role in England of "John Morley & some strong peers and bishops" and the possibility of America's "taking a hand." In December, Clemens was planning to "give a talk on the Congo question" and still hoped "to unseat Leopold."[54] But by 8 January, Clemens had become profoundly discouraged because "the American people unbacked by the American government cannot achieve reform in the Congo"—so he had concluded after his last visit to the State Department some weeks earlier.[55] Moreover, he could not "make a second step" in the "Congo matter" because that would compel further steps—and unlike E.D. Morel, head of the Congo Reform Association, he was not equipped with sufficient "energy, brains, diligence, concentration, persistence."[56] Even so, Clemens in his seventy-first year did not give up easily. As he told Dr. Thomas Barbour in a letter of early February 1906, he had visited Bacon and Root in Washington a week earlier. They had told him that the U.S. government was so entirely outside the Congo matter that it could not move, or second any other nation's move, without laying itself open to the charge of "undiplomatic intrusion."[57] The clinching argument of the State Department people had been that John Hay, dead since July, had held this view and had left it on record. Clemens, an old friend and true admirer of Hay, unhappily agreed.

But within months of Mark Twain's giving up his campaign, so angry and frustrated that he could not bear to read or even think about King Leopold, the President quietly reversed United States policy. In December 1906 he wrote the British Foreign Secretary, Sir Edward Grey, in open support of Congo reform, saying he was "moved by the deep interest shown by all classes of the American people in the amelioration of conditions in the Congo State."[58] Roosevelt's letter, Leopold himself believed, marked the turning point in Congo reform; the Belgian parliament took over control of the Congo from Leopold in 1908.

The supreme irony in all this is that Mark Twain seems never to have known about Roosevelt's changing U.S. policy or the eventual success of the reform movement he had so passionately committed himself to. Nor did he realize that his "fury of generous indignation" in the pamphlet and his talks with the President and the State Department people *had* truly helped to relieve Leopold's wretched

Congolese subjects.[59] Clemens was a wrathy but also a just man. Had he known about it, he would surely have esteemed Theodore Roosevelt highly for this action, no matter what else TR had done.

The Gorki affair forms a kind of pendant to any account of Mark Twain's hope for revolution in Russia. Maxim Gorki, Russian Writer and revolutionary, was warmly received in the United States in the spring of 1906. Howells, Mark Twain, Finley Peter Dunne, Jane Addams, and others formed a committee to raise money for revolutionary purposes, and at a dinner for Gorki on 11 April, Mark Twain spoke briefly but fervently on helping to "give the persecuted people of the Czar's domain the same measure of freedom that we enjoy." A few days later, however, the newspapers discovered that Gorki was living not with his wife but with a Russian actress, Mme. Andreieva—and Howells and Mark Twain with some embarrassment concluded that Gorki had badly misjudged the American public and largely wrecked his mission. Gorki might just as well have appeared in public in his shirt-tail, so Clemens concluded.[60] Theodore Roosevelt on the other hand curtly refused an audience to Gorki at the White House. He despised Gorki's political ideas as those of "the fool academic revolutionist," a revolter against order as well as tyranny in governmental matters, and in domestic matters a rebel against "ordinary decencies and moralities."[61]

It is apparent, then, that Mark Twain differed often and sometimes violently, in print and privately, with President Roosevelt on the war of the U.S. in Cuba and the Philippines, of England against the Boer Republics of South Africa, of the European powers against China during the Boxer Rebellion, of the revolution in Panama, and of Russia and Japan. He held, extravagantly enough, that TR was insane in several ways and "insanest upon war and its supreme glories."[62]

Clemens was critical of TR as well on such domestic issues as the tariff, the recession of 1907, Executive Order 78, and even the coining of gold double-eagles without the inscription "In God We Trust." Most seriously, Mark Twain faulted the President for inviting the Negro educator Booker T. Washington to lunch at the White House and for prejudicing, as he saw it, the trial of a black army regiment at Brownsville, Texas.

What Mark Twain thought in 1901 at the time of Roosevelt's

inviting Washington to lunch at the White House is not certain. What Mark Twain recalled in the Autobiographical Dictation of July 1908 is this: to make a big sensation Mr. Roosevelt invited a Negro to the White House—a man "worth a hundred Roosevelts"—only to face deep disapproval from the southern half of the country. When they were together a little later to receive honorary degrees from Yale, the President asked Clemens if he had not done right in inviting Booker Washington to lunch. Mark Twain had replied that it was a private citizen's right to invite whom he pleased to his table—but that a "president's liberties were more limited."[63] The invitation, Mark Twain believed, was purely, mistakenly, political.

Shortly after it happened, in late 1906—a clash between black soldiers of the 25th Colored Infantry and white townspeople in Brownsville, Texas—Mark Twain told an interviewer that his daughter Jean had written to ask if the dishonorable discharge of all the colored soldiers was not wrong. He had replied that he had as yet no opinion because he had not mastered the facts of the case.[64] By mid-July 1908, however, Clemens was persuaded that the President, seeking to regain favor in the South, had treated the clash of black soldiers and white civilians from the beginning as a "conspiracy" on the part of the soldiers. Unable to convict some of the soldiers, the President himself in effect convicted the entire command and discharged them from the army "without honor."[65] Understandably, neither the White House luncheon nor Brownsville is mentioned in TR's Autobiography. But historically speaking it must be noted that in 1972, Dorsie W. Willis, one of the last surviving members of the 25th Colored Infantry, was given an honorable discharge by the army to replace the discharge "without honor." Willis also received $25,000 compensation from the Congress of the United States.[66]

How then may we interpret and evaluate this sketch by Mark Twain of Theodore Roosevelt, his character and his career as politician and statesman? The spirit is of course the spirit of the satirist. The technique is sometimes deflationary, as in Daumier; more often broad caricature, as in the cartoons of Clemens' friend, Thomas "Nasty" Nast; rarely, grotesque and despairing, as in Goya. There are several occasions, I believe, when Mark Twain loses control, so that the reader tends to sympathize with the subject of the satirical portrait, Roosevelt, rather than the sketcher, Mark Twain. This is often due to Clemens' sense of absolute freedom in the Autobiographical Dictation, his awareness that he is writing for some future reader when the persons treated will be long since dead. The practice is of a piece with his life-long habit of writing angry letters—and then never sending them. That is, many of these excesses in Mark Twain's depiction of Roosevelt would be erased or modified in work designed for publication. Nevertheless, Clemens was a skilled rhetorician who spoke his mind rather often, publicly, about the public Roosevelt, and even his unpublished excesses are interesting. As Howells once remarked in a letter to his friend, "I never knew a man to let himself loose as you do," to the utter delight, he added, of the entire Howells family.[67] Finally Clemens may have kept to the end some liking for Roosevelt as an individual, a private person face to face—though this on balance remains ambiguous. And it seems certain he would have praised TR for the official move against King Leopold—had he known of it. But for Roosevelt the expansionist, the big game hunter, the army colonel who could never forget San Juan Hill, the "Tom Sawyer" show-off, the ambitious politician, Mark Twain saved some of his very sharpest strokes of the pen.

4. TR AND FINLEY PETER DUNNE, "MR. DOOLEY":
"He was my most cherished source of copy"

Just as "Mark Twain" is a pseudonym and a mask for Samuel L. Clemens, so "Mr. Dooley" is the mask for Finley Peter Dunne. In this eighth decade of the twentieth century, Mark Twain is almost universally known, and Howells' reputation and writing are familiar at least to students of American culture, but F.P. Dunne, when he is remembered, is remembered only vaguely as the creator of "Martin Dooley," a bartender who comments shrewdly in a distinct Chicago Irish brogue on affairs of the day. Thirty years younger than Howells and Mark Twain, Dunne was enormously popular for more than twenty-five years, from the time he first created Dooley in the early 1890s to the opening of World War I.[1] He wrote some seven hundred "Mr. Dooley" sketches which were widely syndicated.[2] Whether F.P. Dunne will find a lasting place in American letters is uncertain. But the effort to place him goes on; and in his own time—it is worth observing—Mark Twain and Howells valued him greatly.

So it was that from the mid-1890s to the beginning of the first World War, "Mr. Dooley" found the doings and sayings of Theodore Roosevelt a rich mine of humor and satire. "Tiddy Rosenfelt," as Mr. Dooley liked to call Roosevelt, fascinated the columnist in his always vigorous views about the Anglo-Saxon alliance, politics and government, trusts and labor and strikes, blacks and minorities, women and marriage and children, the strenuous life, and war and expansion. By 1907 Dunne was writing the President to apologize for his "recent unmannerly jibes and jeers" and to explain that he counted TR his "most valuable asset." In his inventory of assets he listed Roosevelt at 75 percent—and Root, Taft, the German emperor, current topics, and the like all that remained.[3] But the entire relation between the two men curiously mixes distrust and admiration in often unequal parts. Dunne was a self-made Irish newspaperman, who could not help being impressed by the Roosevelts' Harvard, Dutch-patroon background—and who eventually sent a son to Groton with TR's backing. But, until late in their acquaintance, Dunne was acutely aware that he had to stand back from TR in order to preserve his independence as a popular commentator; and he never did come to agree with Roosevelt on a number of issues, such as war and expansion.

Or perhaps I should say that "Mr. Dooley" rather than Dunne kept his own counsel, for the Dooley mask was indispensable. "Kipling's like me, Hinnissy," says Dooley, "When I want to say anything lib-lous, I stick it on to me Uncle Mike."[4] With a straight man, Hennessy, and occasionally an ignorant learned man, Hogan, for audience, Dunne could give Dooley's dramatic monologues the form of satire, droll mimicry, fables, tall tales, or rollicking comedy, with every so often a witty maxim that newspaper readers would delightedly quote to their friends.[5] Nevertheless, speaking through the character of Mr. Dooley presented a problem for Dunne of which he was well aware; readers, as time passed, were sure to find the Irish dialect more and more difficult to the eye and ear. Howells raised the question early, asking Dunne in print when he would discard the dialect mask and come into the open "with a bold, vigorous, and incisive satire of our politicians and their methods."[6] The Chicago Irish dialect thus presented only minor difficulties to the contemporary, local readers of Mr. Dooley's columns; but it created larger difficulties for the national audience. And for readers decades later, it poses a major problem. How to resolve it? Even though we may miss certain delectable puns, as for instance, the "Anglo-Saxon 'liance' "[7] or the flavor and lilt of the Irish brogue, rewriting Mr. Dooley into simple American English is probably the best solution, as Dunne himself recognized.[8] So, with a few noted exceptions, I have normalized quotations from Mr. Dooley's essays.

We may begin our portrait by tracing the slow-to-develop friendship of Dunne and Theodore Roosevelt. As Dunne recalled, his first acquaintance with Colonel Roosevelt grew out of an article of November 1899 by no means friendly to TR. Dunne had a picture in his mind of a dude rancher, "noisy, something of a bully, class proud, who pretended to a sentiment of democracy that he by no means

Dooley

Philosopher

felt."[9] Consequently, when *The Rough Riders*, TR's account of his regiment's fighting in Cuba, came to Peter Dunne's desk, the humorist let himself go. Mr. Dooley declares of the book: " 'Tis The Account of the Destruction of Spanish Power in the Ant Hills [the Antilles], as it fell from the lips of Tiddy Rosenfelt and was took down by his own hands." TR, says Dooley, tells how he raised a regiment of fellow hunters from the "large but violent West" and how on the transport going to "Cubia,"

> I would stand beside one of these rough men treating him as an equal, which he was in everything but birth, education, rank, and courage, and together we would look up at the admirable stars . . . and quote the bible from Walt Whitman, he says. Honest, loyal, true-hearted lads, How kind I was to them, he says.

Then after taking charge of the entire army, Dooley relates how Colonel Roosevelt charged up San Juan Hill, killing a Spanish soldier and making the soldier's family, in far off Catalonia, happy with the thought that their representative had been killed "by the future governor of New York." Hennessy protests to Mr. Dooley that it's surely all right for "Tiddy Rosenfelt" to blow his own horn. True for you, responds Dooley; no man that bears a grudge against himself will ever become governor; and if Teddy did it all, he ought to say so and relieve the suspense. But, he concludes with a fine snapper, "If I was him I'd call the book 'Alone in Cubia.' "[10] The phrase swept across the country on a wave of laughter.

Roosevelt immediately wrote Dunne a letter expressing his regret that his family and friends were delighted with Dunne's review of his book, and asking the reviewer to pay him a visit.[11] Dunne responded with a touch of blarney that if he were losing a target and gaining a friend, he was content.[12] Many years later, he concluded about TR that no man could take a joke on himself with better grace.[13] Yet Roosevelt, admitting to an intimate friend that Dooley's article was "exceedingly bright," also conceded, "How he does get at any joint in the harness!"[14]

The humorist never really got acquainted with Roosevelt until the Republican convention in June 1900. The Republican boss of New York state, Tom Platt, wanting to rid himself of TR as governor, urged Hanna and McKinley to sidetrack Roosevelt into the vice-presidential candidacy. While Roosevelt was weighing the decision

46

very carefully, Dunne interviewed him and became the first to learn that TR would run. Thus, TR gave Dunne his second (and final) scoop as a journalist.[15]

Dunne and Augustus St. Gaudens had lunch with TR on a New York train in May 1901. Roosevelt invited Dunne to visit at Oyster Bay on 4 July and Dunne sent regrets.[16] But after the assassination of McKinley when Roosevelt became President, Dunne did go to Washington, in November, for dinner and joked with his host about their dividing his royalties.[17] The acquaintance of the two men grew rapidly after Dunne's marriage to Margaret Abbot in December 1902: TR impulsively invited Dunne and his bride to a reception and supper at the White House the day after they were married.[18] Something of the growing warmth between the two men is even evident in what Mr. Dooley had to say currently about the President's swearing. A trolley driver had heavily bumped the presidential carriage, throwing him to the pavement and provoking a burst of startled, direct curses from TR. The swearing came, Mr. Dooley said, straight from the heart, and "That's one reason I think a lot of us likes Tiddy Rosenfelt that wouldn't ever be suspected of voting for him. When he does any talking . . . he talks at the man in front of him" and uses "words suited to the crisis."[19]

Through 1904, 1905, and 1906, correspondence and visits and encounters were constant. Dunne and his wife must come to the White House and talk literature, Rollo Dunne must be enrolled at Groton, Dunne's view that the Irish do the work in American politics but reap few of the rewards must be refuted at length—so TR urged. In his turn Dunne defends his association with Lincoln Steffens and David G. Phillips, Norman Hapgood and Robert Collier, "muckrakers," and denies any link to or anything but dislike for William Randolph Hearst.[20] In 1907, Dunne summed up his feeling for the President this way, in a letter:

> My personal experience in the country tells me that the general feeling toward you and your administration is one of good-humored affection. People talk about you in the way I think you like best—as the boys in the Army talked about "old Grant," or as people out in Illinois talked about Lincoln. They never speak of you except as "Teddy." They like bantering about you if it isn't ill-natured—that they won't have. I am never conscious of ill-nature in writing about you . . . quite the opposite. . . .[21]

In 1909, however, in the unsigned column of the *American Magazine* called "In the Interpreter's House," Dunne more openly revealed his own still mixed view of the complex man then leaving the presidency. As TR was going off to hunt big game in Africa, Dunne began his farewell editorial by joking that the African flies that bit the President would be less likely to spread sleeping sickness than they would St. Vitus' dance among the population. He has, the editorialist asserts, "made Washington news as interesting as the sporting news" and has brought things to a human plane in the capitol because he is a "born politician." "I have never been a thick-and-thin Roosevelt supporter" and "have been against him in about fifty per cent. of the things he has done," the anonymous writer admits. He finds TR's lapses into epithets and his wretched bad taste and coarse abuse and low style highly objectionable. But the reactions of Roosevelt's enemies measure his effectiveness. He has earned devotion from the young, and broken the allegiance of Irish citizens to the Democratic party, and been the "youngest man of fifty I have ever seen." "I feel that he will be missed," Dunne concludes, "and I am quite sure that when he takes his gun in hand and dives into the forest there will be an almost universal shout of: 'Good-by, Teddy, take keer of yourself.' "[22]

In politics, Mr. Dooley like his creator considered Roosevelt "a born politician." He followed TR's political campaigns with a satirical warmth and expertise first roused by the ward politics of Archer Road in Chicago in the 1890s. Mr. Dooley's satirical stance was of course neither Republican nor Democrat nor even liberal reformist (though it comes closest to this last). No good barten and no popular commentator could afford party views, it goes without saying. But in fact Dunne and Dooley were both rather often subject to Celtic gloom, if not despair, and they simply did not believe in politics, much as they might enjoy following them.

Dunne's fascination with Roosevelt as politician began, as we have seen, in the pre-convention interview of 1900 when Roosevelt gave Dunne a scoop, announcing he would run as McKinley's vice-presidential candidate. That fascination continued through the summer as TR electioneered vigorously throughout the west while McKinley sat on his front porch in Ohio. "If there is any one running in this campaign but my friend Tiddy Rosenfelt," observed Mr.

Dooley in October, "I'd like to know who it is," for Mack is silent, Bryan is visiting his party ancestors' tombs, and Adlai Stevenson is no athlete. Says Dooley, " 'Tis Tiddy alone that's running, and he ain't running, he's galloping."[23] Glory be, cries Dooley, I'd like to be along where he goes "relieving the gloom of the campaign with a bit of real old-fashioned politics." Hennessy interjects his opinion that TR will need a rest cure when he's through; but Dooley concludes, "He expects to be elected."[24] Little wonder that after the election TR told Dunne how much he had enjoyed the piece on his Western trip and invited Dunne to Oyster Bay.[25]

In September, less than two months before election day, Mr. Dooley was in high spirits, remarking that the campaign would soon liven up. "I begin to see signs of the good times coming again," he asserted. It was only the other day that his friend "Tiddy" opened the battle mildly by insinuating that Democrats were liars, horse thieves, and anarchists. " 'Tis true he apologized for that by explaining that he didn't mean all Democrats but only those that wouldn't vote for Mack but I think he'll take the copper off before many weeks." As for McKinley, reports Mr. Dooley, "Tiddy has made application to the national committee for the use of Mack as a sounding board."[26]

In the next year, 1902, Dunne wrote a brilliant essay twitting the President for trying to appoint a killer to a peace officer's job in Arizona, and challenging the dime novel myth of the West as the place of "Strenuous Life and Sudden Death." The President rather than an eastern "lunger" had wanted to appoint "Tarantula Jake, the whirlwind of Zuma Pass," the "quick-drawing, readily passionate, hammerless gun firing Terror of the Desert." But the Senate would not approve TR's candidate. Mr. Dooley laughs at TR again for dropping in on a conference of Rough Riders and cabinet officers who were considering an excursion to Boston to shoot up anti-imperialist "saloons." Mr. Dooley ponders for a moment a westerner's opinion that people who kill each other are not considered respectable in Tucson any more than they would be in Oyster Bay, only with the finest irony to reject so foolish a notion.[27]

Roosevelt's relatively quiet behavior during the dull Republican convention and campaign of 1904[28] inspired in Mr. Dooley one of his wildest fantasies. "Tiddy Rosenfelt has put in an application to join the Quaker Church," declares Mr. Dooley; "He has burned his suit of khaki and beaten his sword into a ploughshare. . . . Secretary Cortelyou authorizes me to deny that the President was ever at San Juan Hill." "A day at Oyster Bay passes like a dream," reports Dooley: the President breakfasts on Quaker Oats, spends the morning in prayer, lunches with his pastor, devotes a few hours to archery and bean bag, sups on popcorn and a dish of tea, and after reading Longfellow aloud and saying family prayers "retires to well-earned slumber."[29] This from the inventor of the strenuous life? A dream indeed!

Mr. Dooley's last major comment on Roosevelt in politics does not mention his name, but the Roosevelt presence may be felt in every line. Writing about the coming Republican convention of 1912, and thinking of the struggle between Taft and LaFollette and Roosevelt, Mr. Dooley predicted that the convention would prove "a combination of the Chicago fire, Saint Bartholomew's massacre, the battle of the Boyne, the life of Jessie James, and the night of the big wind." In response to Hennessy's question, is he going, Dooley responds: "Of course I'm going! I haven't missed a riot in this neighborhood in forty years, and unless I'm deceived by the venal Republican press this one will rejoice the heart."[30] It is also revealing that Dunne should privately support Roosevelt first as a Republican and then as a Progressive, whereas Mr. Dooley took all the campaigning in ironic stride. Dooley was feeling very uneasy, he confesses, until he read the newspapers and discovered that it was not his pants but the republic that was on fire and doomed to destruction—again.[31]

If Mr. Dooley was able to take a cool view of American national politics, he was correspondingly hot in his comments on England and the "Anglo-Saxon Lieance," especially as he suspected Roosevelt of pro-English sympathies. Dunne's animus first appears in a piece of 1898 called "On the Anglo-Saxon," which claims that McKinley is an Anglo-Saxon "whose folks come from County Armagh"; "Teddy Roosevelt is another Anglo-Saxon, . . . and I'm one of the hottest Anglo-Saxons that ever came out of Anglo-Saxony."[32] Similarly, Dooley reviews Rudyard Kipling's newest poem "The Truce of the Bear," which warns of Russian treachery, by getting Father Kelly to write as good a poem on the perilous truce of the British lion. Father Kelly's parody of Kipling ends: "Over and over the story: Beware of the grand flimflam, / There is no truce with

Gazabo, the lion that looks like a lamb."[33] An even more intense small drama grows out of Lord Charles Beresford's speaking tour of the U.S. designed to cement the " 'liance" of the United States and England. Mr. Dooley links Beresford with Rudyard Kipling and Roosevelt as Anglo-Saxons and "whelps of the old lion" ready to go out together and conquer the world—to spread the light of civilization everywhere. Dooley makes the prospect revolting through Beresford's patronizing, even insulting, remarks about the United States.

But the bitterest column on American-English relations that Dunne ever wrote followed Roosevelt's election in November 1904. Congratulations poured in on TR for this "Anglo-Saxon" triumph, especially from England. Ambassador Choate, summoned by the King, says Dooley, "came as fast as his hands and knees would carry him." Dooley then reports the wild approval of one of the English papers thus:

> Thaydoor Rosenfelt is not a statesman in th' English sinse. He wud not compare with our Chamberlains or aven Markses. He is of more vulgar type. Judged be th' English standards, he is a coorse an'oncultivated man. But in America he stands high f'r good taste an' larnin'. He regards his iliction as a great triumph f'r th' Anglo-Saxon race.

As if this were not enough, Mr. Dooley reveals at length how the Irish politician Casey does the leg work and gets out the vote for Judge Silas Higgins, who is elected. But the president-elect gives cabinet jobs to Peabody Perkins and Ponsonby Sanderson—and when Casey asks for places for a few of his campaign workers, the president-elect refers him to the civil service commission, which has charge of the "day laborers." In short, says Mr. Dooley, the Irish do the leg work in politics and they play the football at Harvard and Yale and they do the fighting when fighting is to be done—but Anglophile Americans get the political rewards and honors.[34]

Dunne was plainly angry. Mr. Dooley had presented a strong case. Just how strong may be inferred from the long personal letter that President Roosevelt at once wrote to Dunne, acknowledging his prestige as a "laughing philosopher" and as "a force that counts," but protesting his "very wrong-headed article" and hinting that it might count "on the side of certain ugly and unpleasant tendencies in American life." TR insists that he rewards political workers without regard to race or ethnic strain but defends the descendants of old colonial stock as well. He feels, he says, a "sincere friendliness" for England.[35]

Dunne replied that he liked "straight Americans" but not "dilute Englishmen"—New York dudes and enfeebled literary men from Cambridge and New Haven. Above all he wondered that Roosevelt could hold any sentiment of friendliness for the English government. But he concluded by expressing his pleasure that the "Irish vote" went for TR and declaring that he was sending his son to Groton.[36]

Not all of Dunne's response to Roosevelt's acts and speeches was of course so sharply critical as this comment on the Anglo-Saxon alliance. In the fall of 1902, the United Mine Workers went out on strike, management refused to arbitrate, and the people of the country were threatened with a cold hard winter. George Baer, the leader of the operators, smugly declared in a letter: "The rights and interests of the laboring man will be protected and cared for—not by the labor agitators, but by the Christian men to whom God in His infinite wisdom has given the control of the property interests of the country. . . ."[37] Such arrogance drew a quick rejoinder from Mr. Dooley. "What do you want with coal," he cries to Hennessy; "Everybody will have plenty of fuel this winter. The rich can burn with indignation, thinking of the wrongs inflicted on capital, the middle or middlin' class will be marching with the militia, and the poor can fight among themselves and burn the babies." Mr. Dooley represents Baer, the agent of Divine Providence, as shouting:

> Down with the fire department! I've got some gunpowder in my cellar. I'll touch a match to it. I'm uncomfortable in summer. I'll take my clothes off and go for a walk. The sign above the door belongs to me. I'll loosen it so it will fall down on the top of your head. You want to go to sleep at night. I'm going to have a brass band serenade me. I own a gun. I think I'll shoot my property into you. Get out of the way, for here comes property, drunk and raising Cain. . . .[38]

In this dangerous impasse, President Roosevelt, with the aid of J.P. Morgan, cajoled Baer and the operators into settling the strike through a commission (including Grover Cleveland) and a bit of verbal legerdemain. It was splendid proof of TR's political savvy. He told Dunne in a letter that the final negotiations had been "screaming comedy."[39] Dunne responded with relieved congratulations. He had tried more than once, he said, to deal with the strike situation as a comedy but had had to give it up. "I hope," he wrote, "you hear at least the echoes of the enthusiastic praise that is on everybody's lips, of your management of the crisis. The way you gave the operators the commission they wanted, and the commissioners you wanted yourself would make Cardinal Rampolla weep with envy. It was a great triumph for you and good humor, which is the heart of patience and the eye of diplomacy."[40] Dunne's admiration for Roosevelt's extraordinary feat in settling the coal strike of 1902 never abated, even though he observed in his memoirs that TR repaid J.P. Morgan a hundred times over when "with utter disregard for the statutes" he permitted Morgan to take over the Tennessee Coal and Iron Company in the depression of 1907.[41]

Although the evidence is rather scattering, Mr. Dooley tended to find humorous Roosevelt's divided attitude toward the trusts and big business on the one hand and organized labor on the other. He was, for example, vastly amused by the cautious verbosity of the new President's first message to Congress, on 5 December 1901. The trusts, says Mr. Dooley, reporting the President's remarks, are "hideous monsters built up by the enlightened enterprise of the men that have done so much to advance progress in our beloved country. . . . On one hand I would stamp them under foot; on the other hand not so fast. What I want more than the busting of the trusts is to see my fellow countrymen happy and contented. I wouldn't have them hate the trusts. The haggard face . . . that marks the enemy of trusts is not to my taste. Leave us be merry about it and jovial and affectionate. Leave us laugh and sing the octopus out of existence."[42] Not long after this satirical report, Mr. Dooley again mocked the Rooseveltian balancing act. He, Dooley, did not care "whether the trusts is abolished as Tiddy Rosenfelt would like to have them or encouraged to go on with their nefarious but magnificent enterprises as the President would like."[43] When Upton Sinclair published *The Jungle* in 1906, a novel protesting the power of the meat-packing trust, Mr. Dooley reported President Roosevelt's reaction in a bit of horrified farce, thus:

"Tiddy" was toying with a light breakfast and idly turning over the pages of the new book with both hands. Suddenly he rose from the table, and crying: "I'm poisoned," began throwing sausages out of the window. The ninth one struck Senator Beveridge on the head and made him a blond. It bounced off, exploded, and blew a leg off a secret-service agent, and the scattered fragments destroyed a row of old oak-trees. . . . Since this the President, like the rest of us, has become a vegetarian.

Hennessey says indignantly that the government ought to make the packers eat their own meat—but, counters Dooley, it can't do that because the Constitution forbids cruel and unusual punishments.[44] In general, though Dunne never lost his sympathy for the hod carrier or the slag-heap shoveler, Mr. Dooley approximated the Rooseveltian position between labor and the trusts. Dooley, of the unfortunate middle class, finds that he has to furnish cards and refreshments to the two opponents. " 'Let's play without a limit,' says Labor. 'It's Dooley's Money.' 'Go as far as you like with Dooley's money,' says Capital. 'What have you got?' 'I've got a straight to Roosevelt,' says Labor. 'I've got you beat,' says Capital. 'I've got a Supreme Court full of injunctions.' " Capital and labor are in fact so close together in their present clinch, says Dooley, that the people between them are being crushed.[45] Dooley's distrust of the injunction fairly represents the President's warning of possible abuse of that power, in his Congressional messages of December 1905 and 1906.[46]

Rather closely linked to Dunne's views of TR on the trusts and labor are his opinions on immigrants and on anarchists. In a 1902 column, Mr. Dooley observed that Congress apparently intended to strengthen the immigration laws to keep out anarchists and paupers. A Nicaraguan canal, the Monroe doctrine, irrigation in the West, the Indian question do not concern him a bit, says Dooley, but immigration, now, is different. It used to be that America was the refuge of the oppressed of all the world, even of Dooley and the Irish day laborer, whom those "stern and rockbound" Pilgrim fathers, the "Rosenfelts and the Lodges beat . . . by at least a boat length." But, argues Dooley with vivid irony, the immigrants now, those "paupers and anarchists," don't assimilate with the country. Perhaps on the other hand the country is trying to digest too much rich food, hints the humorist; perhaps it ought to leave off trying to digest Rockefeller and try a simple diet of Schwartzmeister instead. Hennessey protests that immigrants are anarchists, the "scum of the earth."

"They may be that," counters Dooley, "but we used to think they was the cream of civilization."[47]

In the matter of minorities and what Kipling called "lesser breeds without the law," Martin Dooley tended to differ from Roosevelt. Although he recognized the national prejudice against Negroes, he did not share it fully; and as a self-conscious Irish Catholic commentator on world affairs, he sided often with the underdog. Thus in 1899 Mr. Dooley sardonically tells the Filipino "naygurs" that after liberating them from Spain, we Americans now "propose for to learn ye the uses of liberty," "ye miserable, childish-minded apes."[48] He defends the Boers in South Africa against the British.[49] And in a piece on "The Chinese Situation" he imagines himself in the shoes of "Hop Lung Dooley" and asserts, "if I was a Chinaman . . . and was living at home, I'd tuck my shirt into my pants, put my braid up in a net, and take a fall out of the invader if it cost me my life."[50] Roosevelt's response to the thrusts of Mr. Dooley was predictably in opposition but admiring. He wrote to Dunne, "Your delicious phrase about 'Take up the white man's burden and put it on the coon' exactly hit off the weak spot in my own theory."[51] Presumably Mr. Dooley meant that the colonial peoples ought to manage their own affairs: whereas Roosevelt seemed to think that such self-government would be a long time in coming.

The greatest single social controversy of Roosevelt's career arose in October 1901 when the new President invited Booker T. Washington, the Negro educator, to dinner at the White House to discuss appointments and Southern politics.[52] The response of Southern newspapers was violent, like that of Dooley's straight man, Hennessy, who was deeply offended by the President's "having a coon to dinner at the White House," as he put it. Mr. Dooley sagely predicted the invitation would ruin President Teddy's chances in the South: "Thousands of men who wouldn't have voted for him under any circumstances," opined Dooley, "has declared that under no circumstances would they now vote for him." He feels sure that there cannot be a "Crow Heaven" and wonders whether in the heavenly realm they may not get on without "race supreemacy." Mr. Dooley admits that he won't have black men in his bar because even though he and "Tiddy" are public servants, the public won't accept blacks socially. Even so, Dooley avers, he would do something for the Negro: he would give him the only right he needs, "the right to live," and thus he might make something of himself.[53] Several years later, Martin Dooley returned to the issue in a column called "The Race Question."[54] His mood was even more somber. "Teddy Roosevelt's idea is to glad-hand [the Negro] up to a higher plane . . . to give him a job and have him up to the White House for dinner"—so writes the humorist. But the trouble is "the higher you boost the negro, the farther he has to fall when he gets about two blocks south of the White House.[55] Dooley ends his column bitterly: "The President of the United States must know that we will defend white supremacy to the last drop of their blood"[56]—that is to say, of Negro blood.

During the fall of 1906, President Roosevelt defended the treaty rights of Japanese citizens in California against such discriminatory acts as the San Francisco schoolboard's ordering them to attend their own segregated schools.[57] The resultant friction and fear provided Mr. Dooley with a chance to satirize American distrust of foreigners, especially of Californians' fear of the Japanese. His burlesque scenario of the threatening future in "The Japanese Scare" included the Japanese landing in Boston to scalp the wigs off the descendants of John Hancock and Sam Adams; Teddy Roosevelt's being discovered "under a bed with a small language book trying to learn to say 'Spare me' in the Japanese tongue"; and (two hundred years into the future) the children of Kenosha, Wisconsin, eating their milk with chop sticks.[58]

It was one of Roosevelt's profoundest convictions that married women and men, especially the well-educated, had an obligation to produce children. When a senior at Harvard, TR had written his dissertation on "The Practicability of Equalizing Men and Women Before the Law" and had advocated woman suffrage and women's rights, beginning with property rights. But from the turn of the century on, Roosevelt lamented the declining birthrate among the "Anglo-Saxon nations," praised the parents of large families, condemned birth control and divorce, and considered what he called "willful sterility" in marriage a hideous form of vice."[59] Such views provided Dunne with rich satirical opportunities. In a piece on "The American Family" of 1906, Mr. Dooley observes that "Dock Eliot" of Harvard thinks the race is dying out and Teddy Roosevelt is worried about it. All that Eliot and Roosevelt have to do to learn differently, however, is to come out to Archer Road some summer afternoon, to see that "the race is running easy and coming strong."[60] A good deal less genially, Mr. Dooley satirizes the President's wanting to re-introduce the whipping-post as punishment for wife-beaters. He is right, says Dooley the bachelor, "I'm in favor of having wife-beaters whipped, and I'll go further and say that 'twould be a good thing to have every married man scourged about once a month." In fact, argues Dooley, he looks forward to having a government whipping post with an American flag on top of it in every American city. The cat-o'-nine tails can have the federal seal of the U.S. on it—and "Love one another" engraved on the handle. In this essay on "Corporal Punishment" Dunne is truly penetrating on the "habit of cruelty" among lynchers of black men, wardens, hanging judges, and schoolmasters. He has Mr. Dooley conclude that "there ain't a hair's difference between a blackguard who beats his wife and a government that beats its children."[61]

"The strenuous life" is of course a familiar phrase and concept in the life and thought of TR. First voiced in a vigorous speech in Chicago in 1899 it relates closely to Roosevelt's advocacy of physical fitness, of the military virtues, of large families, and of national expansion. It appeared as a book of essays the following year.[62] It provided Peter Dunne with a broad target for burlesque admiration and satire, for although he was ten years younger than Roosevelt, Dunne did not in the least care for hiking, riding, hunting, wrestling, swimming, tennis, and the rest: what he liked above everything was to drink and talk.

The tone for much of Dunne's comment on Roosevelt's strenuosity is set by Mr. Dooley's version of Colonel Roosevelt's western tour in the fall campaign of 1900. The Colonel shakes hands with two hundred thousand Rough Riders in South Dakota, busts an unbustable bronco, brings down the Democratic Committee chairman with a well-aimed shot, and kicks a four-ton boulder out of a Rough Rider friend's mining sluice.[63] After the election, at Thanksgiving, Mr. Dooley gives thanks that he is not, among others, "President Teddy, for when the day is done he can close up shop and relax." But the President cannot escape his duties, Dooley explains to Hennessy:

He has to set up at night steering the stars straight, hoist the sun at the right moment, turn on the hot and cold faucet [of the weather], . . . salt mines with a four years' supply of gold, trap the microbes as they fly through the air and see that ten dollars is equally divided among one hundred men so that each man gets thirty dollars more than any other.

So, declares Mr. Dooley, he is thankful he is not Roosevelt—though he does wish the country might stop growing in width and grow a little more in height.[64] Mr. Dooley's verbal manner of admiration-tinged-with-irony is especially vivid in a column of the same fall of 1901. When Hennessy charges Dooley with being "disrespectful" in speaking of the youngest of the Presidents as "Tiddy," Dooley retorts that he is "affectionate," "familiar," but not "disrespectful"—even though a committee of ferocious clergymen may burn him at the stake for saying so.[65]

A year later, Mr. Dooley described the Roosevelt strenuosity, breadth of interest, and exuberance at Oyster Bay, thus:

> There day by day the head of the nation transacts the nation's business as follows: four A. M., a plunge into the salt, salt sea and a swim of twenty miles; five A. M., horse-back ride, the president instructing his two sons, aged two and four respectively, to jump the first Methodist church without knocking off the shingles; six A. M., wrestles with trained grizzly bear; seven A. M. breakfast; eight A. M., Indian clubs; nine A. M., boxes with Sharkey; ten A. M., beats the tennis champion; eleven A. M., receives a band of rough riders . . . . noon, dinner with Sharkey . . . . [and a wildly variegated group of guests, whose conversation] dealt with art, boxing, literature, horse-breaking, science, shooting, politics, how to kill a mountain lion, diplomacy, lobbying, poetry, the pivot blow, reform, and the campaign in Cuba . . . .

In short, says the humorist, the guests enjoyed an ideal day in the country.[66]

The genial tenor of this column turned to sardonic attack, however, when TR administered a severe reprimand to Lt. General Nelson Miles for commenting adversely in the newspapers on the verdict of a naval board of inquiry. Niles had also protested atrocities committed by American soldiers in the Philippines.[67] Mr. Dooley imagines the scene in the White House in December 1901 as a physical confrontation in which the President administers a severe reprimand to Miles, and a right to the jaw. You've been in the army forty years, says TR to Miles, and you should know that the regular way to criticize a fellow officer is in a round robin letter. (This is of course a sharp thrust at Roosevelt for *his* round robin letter to his military superiors during the war in Cuba.) Miles is booted out of a White House window "pursued by a chandelier," and Mr. Dooley concludes that the art of governing, of making others do what *you* want them to do, is much the same in the Capitol as it is on Archey Road: If you can't do it with a song, "do it with a shovel."[68]

Dunne's considered conclusion in the matter of the vigorous life is best summed up, perhaps, in Mr. Dooley's "Casual Observation" of 1900: "I'd like to tell me frind Tiddy that they'se a strenuse life an' a sthrenuseless life." In 1906 TR preached a related doctrine—what he called "the simple life." Dooley responded, "Tell me, Thaydore Rosenfelt, simple soul, what I must do? . . . Hand out the receipt," and then answered his own question: There is no simple life, there's only life, and life is a kind of obstacle race and "the truth is never simple."[69]

I have observed that Dunne opposed Roosevelt about half the time in the things he did in office. Much, perhaps most, of that opposition came from Dunne's distrust of American policy in the Philippine phase of the Spanish American war, under President McKinley first, then under Roosevelt.

Dunne, as we have seen, chaffed the President good naturedly on many of his beliefs and actions. There was one trait, however, in Roosevelt which Dunne adamantly opposed—that is, his militaristic and imperialistic way of thinking. Once a friend of Dunne's asked him how such an "inveterate enemy of poseurs" was able to enjoy the President's company. Dunne replied that he enjoyed TR's company, every minute of it—except when Roosevelt began to glorify war as a good in itself. Then he had to leave.[70] The record clearly bears this out.

Mr. Dooley's distrust of Vice President Roosevelt on war remained implicit for a time in his criticism of President McKinley's policy in the Philippines—but when Roosevelt became President at McKinley's death and strongly pursued McKinley's war policies, Dunne simply shifted his aim from McKinley to Roosevelt. The issue was drawn early. In January 1899, Mr. Dooley, neatly representing the divided opinions of his fellow countrymen, makes them say to the Filipinos, "We'll treat you the way a father should treat his children if we have to break every bone in your bodies."[71] In the same piece, called "Expansion," Dunne drew a kind of cartoon figure in which the "indulgent parent" is kneeling on the stomach of his adopted child, "while a delegation from Boston"—the New England Anti-Imperialist League—"bastes him with an umbrella." There it stands, Mr. Dooley avows, and "how it will come out I don't know. I'm not much of an expansionist myself." In fact, Dooley confesses in a *Chicago Journal* column of March, " 'Tis sthrange how I've cam'd down since th'war . . . . Whin I think of the gaby I made iv mesilf dancin' ar-round this here bar an hurooin' whiniver I he-erd iv Rosenfelt's charge again Sandago me blood r-runs cold with shame." "Did ye iver set up late at night an' come down in the mornin'," he explains, "feelin' a taste in ye'er mouth like a closed sthreet car on a r-rainy day? That's the way I feel. Was I dhrunk durin' th' war?"[72] Charles Fanning believes that Dooley was strongly pro-war, even a jingo, during the Cuban fighting, partly on the evidence of this confession of war-drunkenness just cited. But Dooley was nothing if not dramatic, and he rarely missed the chance to dramatize, even a change from humorous neutrality to open opposition.

A few months later, Roosevelt wrote to Dunne that *he* was an unabashed Expansionist, capitalizing the E. But Dunne continued his sniping. Observing TR's rough-and-tumble campaign in the West, in October 1900, Mr. Dooley praises the Vice President's rhetorical power: in this way Roosevelt "proves that 'tis by electing himself and the other lad on the ticket, the hydra-headed monster called by the foolish anti-imperialism and by the wise free silver, anarchy, violence, and intolerance can be crushed."[73] At the same time, Mr. Dooley defended the Chinese resistance to the Western powers in the Boxer Rebellion—a grand contest, he called it, be-tween "Western and Eastern civiliezation,"[74] between the infidel Chinese and the Germans bearing the banner of the cross—and the double-cross."[75]

Perhaps the most famous witticism ever pronounced by Mr. Dooley followed the decision of the Supreme Court that the Con-stitution does not follow the flag. In more direct terms, the decision meant that the Filipinos could not vote or have the right of habeas corpus and that they might be taxed without being represented. After poking fun at the justices of the Supreme Court for their erudite opacity in written legal decisions, the bewildered Dooley revealed that he knew just one thing for certain: "No matter whether the constitution follows the flag or not, the supreme court follows the election returns."[76] Popular reverence in the United States for the Supreme Court and its decisions would never be quite the same again.

In "The Philippine Peace" (collected in 1902), Mr. Dooley produced his own version of Governor William Howard Taft's report on pacification of the islands. Despite the fact that the Filipinos have neither the vote nor the right to trial by jury, they love the U.S. government, reports Dooley—because Governor Taft in his report says they do. They raise unmentionable products—which cannot be imported into the United States. The climate is heavenly—though a white man who goes there "seldom returns unless the bereaved family insists." The political situation is good—in that the army converts the heathen by the well-known American water-cure and that the reconcentration camps are thickly populated. In short, says Dooley, "Everywhere happiness, content, love of the stepmother country, except in places where there are people."[77]

At about the same time, Dunne caricatured the President standing once again on top of San Juan hill, sword in hand and gleaming specs on his nose, ending the domination of the beet and beet sugar in the Western world. But if Cuba is free and in trouble, says Dooley, the trouble with the Philippines is the Philippine trouble. Is the trouble "All over"? asks Hennessy. Dooley responds—with characteristic wit, it's "All over."[78]

One of the events in the Philippines that most aroused anti-imperialists like Mark Twain and F.P. Dunne was the manner of General Frederick Funston's capturing the Filipino insurgent leader Emilio Aguinaldo. Subsequently General "Fustian," as Dooley calls him, went on a kind of rampage in Dooley's fantasy. He administered the water-cure to Filipino generals, attacked anti-imperialist leaders, hanged literature and science and the constitution, and wound up arresting anti-administration forces in Washington. The President finally called Funston down, reports Dooley, after the general's fifteenth speech, in which "Fustian" sentenced to death every college professor in the land. Roosevelt's letter in the Dooley-version read:

Dear Fred: My attention has been called to your patriotic utterances in favor of frying Edward Atkinson on his own cook stove. I am informed by my advisers that it can't be done. It won't fry beans. So I am compelled by the regulations of war to give you a good slap. How are you, old comrade-in-arms? You ought to have seen me on the top of San Juan hill. Oh, that was the day! Ever, my dear Fred, reprovingly but lovingly, T. Roosevelt, late Colonel First United States Volunteers Cavalry, better known as the Rough Riders, and ex-officio president of the United States.[79]

We may take as Dunne's last word on the subject of armed conflict a column in 1906 entitled "War" dealing with the Russian-Japanese fighting. Dooley remarks that "War is a fine thing. Or perhaps I'm wrong. Anyhow, it's a strange thing." But fine or wrong or strange, if he had his way, he wouldn't let the common people fight at all. He would match up Nick Romanoff and the Mikado; or Roosevelt, "the American champion who has issued a defy to the world" and the Emperor of Germany; or just officers; or any one seeking to gratify the "heroic spirit." Only one thing, says Mr. Dooley. "Whenever I'm called on to fight for [the old firm of] God and my country, I'd like to be sure the senior partner had been consulted."[80] This column precedes Theodore Roosevelt's act of diplomacy in ending the Russo-Japanese war—a feat that Dunne unlike Mark Twain admired greatly.[81]

In his unfinished reminiscences, F.P. Dunne recalled the "many-sided" Roosevelt genially. "An era ended with his death," he believed, and whatever Elysium his spirit has chosen, it will not be a dull place. "The saints will have to go disguised as boxers, scholars, jockeys, prestidigitators" as well as "minor journalists who see nothing sacrilegious in laughter." Even in a halo, Dunne concludes, "Theodore Roosevelt will be good copy and a good friend."[82] This tribute, however, heart-felt though it may be, does not fully represent the humorous intelligence of Dunne vis-à-vis Roosevelt. Howells came closer to it in reviewing "Mr. Dooley's Musings on Men and Things" in 1903. Dunne is "of the line of great humorists who have not failed us in our crises of folly or misdoing," he said, because "to have one's heart in the right place . . . is indispensable; but to have one's head in the right place, also adds immeasurably to the other advantage."[83] Perhaps Dunne himself came closest to revealing his own unique talent, in a burst of candor on "Things Spiritual" in 1910. Taking off from a news-item that a man in Massachusetts had determined the weight of the soul to be six ounces, Mr. Dooley is moved to say:

> What do I know about anything? . . . I tell you now I don't know anything about anything. I don't like to thrust myself forward. I'm a modest man. Won't somebody else get up? Won't you get up, Teddy Roosevelt? won't you, William Jennings Bryan; won't you, President Eliot; won't you, professors, preachers, doctors, lawyers, editors? Won't anybody get up? Won't anybody say that they don't know anything about anything worth knowing about? Then, by Heavens, I will.

And Mr. Dooley then lectures Hennessy on how little he knows about himself: whether he is gay, or careless, or gloomy, or wretched, or cantankerous or crazy, he is "uncharted." It is certain that F.P. Dunne was often afflicted with Celtic melancholy and that he never lost his taste for the skepticism of Montaigne. This witty skepticism is surely a key to his humor, and what makes him still at his best Roosevelt's "laughing philosopher" and Howells's thoughtful and subtle humorist.[84]

The evidence I have been citing argues that a citizen in the Republic of Letters, American division, can hardly avoid taking views or positions with or against the President *if* the President is as strong and active as Theodore Roosevelt. He may or may not choose to voice or publish them, but he is sure to feel them and they are likely to appear in his work implicitly. If he is a good writer with the instinct of workmanship and the ability to distinguish good from shoddy work, his views of the character and thoughts and actions of a President may therefore be more perceptive, just, truthful than the views of most of us—and so more worthy of attention. Malcolm Cowley in his recent book *And I Worked at the Writer's Trade* says, challengingly, "No complete son-of-a-bitch ever wrote a good sentence." The French expert on the U.S.A., Jean-François Ravel, is equally challenging in his argument that the discovery and exposure of Watergate argued strength, not weakness, in the American democratic process.

I would never claim with P.B. Shelley that "poets are the unacknowledged legislators of the world" or even that if they are not they somehow should be. For the critic-historian this sounds a little too much like crying one's own wares. What I do suggest however, is that

Howells and Mark Twain and F.P. Dunne, individual and different as they were, shared in a strong national tradition of skepticism and humor and satire. They valued "irreverence," to use Mark Twain's word. Their opinions, both sympathetic and condemnatory, of Theodore Roosevelt and his accomplishments were therefore more penetrating on the whole than the judgments of Americans at large.

I wonder, in fact, if this "irreverence" in the face of dubious political policies and actions may not possess value for prediction and the future. All three writers refused to discriminate between the President's ends and his means in "taking Panama," as he phrased his action to students in Berkeley well after the event. The promised restoration to the Panamanians of the canal in the year 2000 now redresses a balance and alters the relation of the United States to South American nations generally. Roosevelt's role in the dismissing of an entire Negro army regiment "without honor" following a clash at Brownsville, Texas, of black soldiers and white townspeople, struck Mark Twain as flatly wrong. One of the Brownsville soldiers still living was given an honorable discharge from the army recently and secured redress—a single small episode but a part of what is still perhaps the American dilemma, delay in securing the civil rights of black citizens. Howells defended the married couple's right to have as few children as they chose against Roosevelt's argument that such Americans would bring on race suicide. Dunne called attention to the large Irish families of Chicago and just laughed. But the probability has now arisen that population increase, not decrease, is more likely to lead to national weakness or disaster. Dunne and Howells and Mark Twain, all three, protested and continued to protest American army policy in the guerilla fighting in the Philippines and violations of the constitution in civil government there. Surely, without such protest Philippine independence would have been delayed even longer and Philippine resistance to the Japanese in World War II might very likely have been less.

The conclusions of Dunne and Howells and Mark Twain concerning Roosevelt now represent, I suggest, "the verdict of history." Or if there is truly no such thing, they anticipate the verdict of the most acute historians. Despite errors of judgment and failures to recognize Roosevelt's great accomplishments in conservation or in curbing the worst abuses of the trusts, or in establishing peace between Japanese and Russians, or in Congo reform, for example, the three writers served and still serve as gadflies of the presidency and the state, as reminders of constitutional principles and civil rights. The literature in which they embodied these values—letters, reviews, essays, interviews, editorials, sketches of character—is varied in form and scattering; but it is memorable as a literature that adjusts, focuses, relates, corrects, sets in proportion. Because it subjects even a President (or especially a President) to the "irreverent" inspection of the satirist and humorist, to his wit and candor, three quarters of a century later it still breathes the breath of life.

ABBREVIATIONS

AL—Autographed letter.
ALS—Autographed letter signed.
Dissertations—F.P. Dunne, *Dissertations by Mr. Dooley* (New York: Harper, 1906).
DLC—Library of Congress
Ellis—Elmer Ellis, *Mr. Dooley's America, A Life of Finley Peter Dunne* (New York: Knopf, 1941).
Fatout—Paul Fatout, ed., *Mark Twain Speaking* (Iowa City: Univ. of Iowa Press, 1976).
FPD—Finley Peter Dunne.
HCL—Harvard College Library
HE Center—Howells Edition Center, Indiana Univ.
Hearts—F.P. Dunne, *Mr. Dooley in the Hearts of his Countrymen* (Boston: Small, Maynard, 1899).
Letters TR—*The Letters of Theodore Roosevelt*, Elting E. Morison, ed. (Cambridge: Harvard Univ. Press, 1951).
LinL—*Life in Letters of William Dean Howells*, Mildred Howells, ed. (New York: Doubleday, 1928).
MH—Harvard Univ. Library.
Mr. Dooley Remembers—*Mr. Dooley Remembers, the Informal Memoirs of Finley Peter Dunne,* Philip Dunne, ed. (Boston: Little, Brown, 1963).
Mr. Dooley Says—F.P. Dunne, *Mr. Dooley Says* (New York: Scribner's, 1910).
Mr. Dooley's Philosophy—F.P. Dunne, *Mr. Dooley's Philosophy* (New York: R.H. Russell, 1900).
MT—Mark Twain, Samuel Langhorn Clemens.
MTA—*Mark Twain's Autobiography*, A.B. Paine, ed. (2 vols., New York: Harper, 1924).

MTE—Mark Twain in Eruption, Bernard DeVoto, ed. (New York: Harper, 1940).

MTHL—Mark Twain-Howells Letters (2 vols., Cambridge: Harvard University Press, 1960). Henry Nash Smith and William M. Gibson, eds.

MTP—Mark Twain Papers, Univ. of California Library, Berkeley.

MWA—American Antiquarian Society, Worcester, Mass.

NAR—North American Review.

NYPL—New York Public Library.

Observations—F.P. Dunne, *Observations of Mr. Dooley* (New York: Harper, 1902).

Opinions—F.P. Dunne, *Mr. Dooley's Opinions* (New York: Harper, 1901).

Peace and War—F.P. Dunne, *Mr. Dooley in Peace and War* (Boston: Small, Maynard, 1899).

SLC—Samuel Langhorn Clemens, "Mark Twain."

TLS—Typed letter signed.

TR—Theodore Roosevelt.

WDH—William Dean Howells.

Works TR—The Works of Theodore Roosevelt, Herman Hagedorn, ed. (New York: Scribner's, 1926).

NOTES

CHAPTER I

1. "Pandora," *Daisy Miller, Pandora* . . . (New York Edition. New York: Scribner's, 1909), XVIII, 131. My thanks to Ernest Samuels, who placed the witticism for me and confirmed Adams as the source, in *The Middle Years* (Cambridge: Harvard Univ. Press, 1965), 168.
2. *New York Times*, 21 Jan. 1977.
3. Emery Neff, *Edwin Arlington Robinson* (New York: Sloane, 1948), 139–41, 166ff; *The Letters of Theodore Roosevelt*, Elting E. Morison, ed. (Cambridge: Harvard Univ. Press, 1951), IV, 1303. Hereafter *Letters TR*.
4. *Roosevelt as the Poets Saw Him*, C.H. Towne, ed. (New York: Scribner's, 1923), 39.
5. Henry F. Pringle, *Theodore Roosevelt, A Biography* (New York: Harcourt, Brace, 1931), 242–44. Hereafter Pringle.
6. 29 June, to Brander Mathews, *Letters TR*, I, 390.
7. Leon Edel, *Henry James the Master: 1901–1916* (Philadelphia: Lippincott, 1972), 265, 267.
8. R.W. Stallman, *Stephen Crane, A Biography* (New York: Braziller, 1968), 219–31, 384, 607 fn 10.
9. *The Works of Theodore Roosevelt*, Herman Hagedorn, ed. (National Edition. New York: Scribner's, 1926), XI, 69. Hereafter *Works TR*.
10. *Roosevelt as the Poets Saw Him*, 117–23.
11. Clyde Dornbusch, "Theodore Roosevelt's Literary Taste and Relationship with Authors," unpubl. doctoral diss., Duke Univ., 1957, 7 Feb. 1917, to E.L. Masters, HCL.
12. Edgar Lee Masters, *Across Spoon River* (New York: Farrar, 1936), 338.
13. H.L. Mencken, *Prejudices Second Series*, "Roosevelt: An Autopsy" (New York: Knopf, 1920).
14. *The New Mencken Letters*, Carl Bode, ed. (New York: Dial, 1977), 96.
15. Ellen Glasgow, *The Woman Within* (New York: Harcourt, Brace, 1954), 208–209.
16. Edith Wharton, *A Backward Glance* (New York: Appleton-Century, 1936), 311–17.

17. R.W.B. Lewis, *Edith Wharton: A Biography* (New York: Harper, 1975), 391–92.
18. *Roosevelt as the Poets Saw Him*, 115–17.

CHAPTER 2

1. "Editor's Study," *Harper's Monthly Magazine*, LXXVII (July 1888), 314–18.
2. "Editor's Easy Chair," *Harper's*, CVII (Nov. 1903), 968.
3. "Editor's Study," *Harper's*, LXXIX (Oct. 1889), 800–805, the first two volumes.
4. "Editor's Study," *Harper's*, LXXXI (Oct. 1890), 800–804.
5. TR to W.D. Howells, 20 Oct. 1890, Harvard Univ. Library, hereafter MH; and Howells Edition Center, Indiana Univ., hereafter HE Center.
6. W.D. Howells to TR, 26 Oct. 1890, Boston, MH, HE Center.
7. Van Wyck Brooks, *Howells, His Life and World* (New York: Dutton, 1959), 202.
8. TR to Brander Mathews, 2 May 1892, quoted in Dornbusch, 214.
9. TR to H.C. Lodge, 11 Oct. 1892, *Letters TR*, I, 292.
10. TR to WDH, 15 Dec. 1892, MH, HE Center.
11. TR to Brander Mathews, 7 Dec. 1894, *Letters TR*, I, 410.
12. TR to Arlo Bates, 29 Sept. 1897, *Letters TR*, I, 694.
13. Hamlin Garland, *Roadside Meetings* (New York: Macmillan, 1930), 328–92.
14. TR to WDH, 6 March 1897, MH, HE Center.
15. *Works TR*, XII, *Literary Essays*, 184, 202. William Henry Harbaugh, *Power and Responsibility, The Life and Times of Theodore Roosevelt* (New York: Farrar, Strauss, 1961), 220–21. Hereafter Harbaugh.
16. Pringle, 472.
17. *Harper's Weekly*, XLVII (7 March 1903), 388–89.
18. *Ibid*.
19. *Mark Twain-Howells Letters*, Henry Nash Smith and William M. Gibson, eds. (Cambridge: Harvard Univ. Press, 1960) II, 673, 682. Hereafter *MTHL*.
20. WDH to Aurelia Howells, 6 Nov. 1898, MH, HE Center.
21. 6 April 1902, TS in HE Center.
22. "Editor's Easy Chair," *Harper's*, CII (April 1901), 805; and *ibid.* (May 1901), 966–67, a review of N.S. Shaler, *The Individual, A Study of Life and Death*.
23. TR to H.C. Lodge, 9 Dec. 1901, *Letters TR*, III, 142.
24. Pringle, 110–11.
25. "Editor's Easy Chair," *Harper's*, CIV (Jan. 1902), 334–38.

26. *Harper's Weekly*, XLVI (8 March 1902), 293.
27. *Ibid.* (7 June 1902), 715.
28. *Ibid.* (28 June 1902), 811.
29. *Ibid.* (19 July 1902), 946.
30. *Ibid.* (12 July 1902), 907.
31. "Editor's Easy Chair," *Harper's*, CIX (Sept. 1904), 642.
32. *Ibid.*, 645.
33. *Ibid.*
34. "Race Patriotism," *Harper's Weekly*, XLVI (10 May 1902), 585.
35. *Ibid.*, XLVIII (27 Feb. 1904), 321.
36. *Ibid.*, XLIX (26 Aug. 1905), 1244.
37. WDH to Aurelia Howells, 31 July 1904, MH, HE Center.
38. WDH to Aurelia Howells, 28 Sept. 1905, MH, HE Center.
39. WDH to Joseph Howells, 28 Sept. 1905, MH, HE Center.
40. WDH to Aurelia Howells, 1 Oct. 1905, MH; and TR to WDH, 2 Oct. 1905, MH, HE Center.
41. WDH to Joseph A. Howells, 16 April 1906, *Life in Letters of William Dean Howells*, Mildred Howells, ed. (New York: Doubleday, 1928), II, 220. Hereafter *LinL*.
42. WDH to TR, 26 Aug. 1906, *LinL*, II, 227–28.
43. TR to WDH, 28 Aug. 1906, MH, HE Center.
44. *Harper's*, CXIII (Sept. 1906), 634–37.
45. *Ibid.*, 634.
46. WDH to C.E. Norton, 6 April 1903, MH, HE Center, partially printed in *LinL*, II, 170–72.
47. "Editor's Easy Chair," *Harper's*, CXXI (Nov. 1910), 957–60.
48. *Ibid.*, CXVII (July 1908), 309–12; WDH to Elizabeth Jordan, 4 July 1906, NYPL, HE Center; 25 Oct. 1905, Filson Club, HE Center.
49. WDH to Joseph A. Howells, 9 Dec. 1906, *LinL*, II, 231; TR to WDH, 26 Dec. 1906, MH, HE Center, and *LinL*, II, 233–34.
50. *Boston Herald* (10 June 1907), 2; WDH to C.E. Norton, 10 June 1907, MH, HE Center; letter of 23 June, *New York Sun*, 26 June 1907.
51. WDH to Henry B. Fuller, 14 March 1909, *LinL*, II, 264, and Robert B. Sinclair, HE Center.
52. Pringle, 243.
53. WDH to F.A. Duneka, 1 June 1910, MWA, HE Center.
54. See *Public Meeting . . . in Memory of Samuel Langhorne Clemens* (New York: American Academy of Arts and Letters, 1922).

CHAPTER 3

1. *Mark Twain's Autobiography*, A.B. Paine, ed. (2 vols., New York: Harper, 1924), I, 290–91. Hereafter *MTA*.
2. *Mark Twain Speaking*, Paul Fatout, ed. (Iowa City: Univ. of Iowa Press, 1976), 345. Hereafter Fatout.

3. Pringle, 474.

4. Fatout, 70th Birthday Speech, 5 Dec. 1905, p. 465.

5. *Mark Twain in Eruption*, Bernard De Voto, ed. (New York: Harper, 1940), 10–12, 17–18. Hereafter *MTE*.

6. *Letters TR*, 16 Feb. 1907, to Kermit Roosevelt, V, 590.

7. *MTA*, I, 287–91.

8. *Ibid.*, 291.

9. A.B. Paine, *Mark Twain, A Biography* (New York: Harper, 1912), IV, 1340.

10. *MTE*, 33–34.

11. *Ibid.*, 1 Nov. 1907, pp. 6, 14, 15, 17, 4–6.

12. *Ibid.*, 49.

13. *Letters TR*, I, 390; V, 137; V, 813; and *Works TR*, XII, *Literary Essays*, 338.

14. *Ibid.*, V, 590, 16 Feb. 1907.

15. Hamlin Hill, *Mark Twain, God's Fool* (New York: Harper, 1973), 88.

16. *Mark Twain's Seventieth Birthday ... Supplement to Harper's Weekly*, 23 Dec. 1905, pp. 2–3.

17. Advertising pamphlet, Collier's, n.d., unpaginated.

18. Fatout, Speech, 19 Sept. 1906, p. 523.

19. *Ibid.*, 7 Dec. 1906, pp. 534–35.

20. *Letters TR*, III, 112, TR to G.F. Becker, 8 July 1901.

21. Anson P. Stokes to Dixon Wecter, 8 Feb. 1949, MTP, quoted in *MTHL*, II, 743.

22. Fatout, 10 Nov. 1900, p. 351.

23. *Nation*, LXXI (29 Nov. 1900), 419.

24. *Ibid.*, 420.

25. Fatout, 4 Jan. 1901, p. 372.

26. *Ibid.*, 23 March 1901, p. 394.

27. "Editor's Easy Chair," *Harper's*, CIII (Aug. 1901), 493–94.

28. MT to TR, 24 Dec. 1901, MS letters DLC. *Macbeth*, I, vii, reads: ". . . this Duncan / Hath borne his faculties so meek, hath been / So clear in his great office, that his virtue / Will plead like angels . . . ."

29. TR to SLC, 28 Dec. 1901, MS in DLC.

30. A tag from Thomas Martin's *Speed the Plough*, V, Sc. 2.

31. William M. Gibson, *The Art of Mark Twain* (New York: Oxford Univ. Press, 1976), 146.

32. *Fables of Man*, John S. Tuckey, ed. (Berkeley: Univ. of California Press, 1972), 405.

33. *Ibid.*, 711.

34. *North American Review*, CLXXIV (May 1902), 613–24. Hereafter *NAR*.

35. *Harper's Weekly*, XLVI (26 April 1902), 542; XLVI (3 May 1902), 550.

36. Louis J. Budd, *Mark Twain, Social Philosopher* (Bloomington: Indiana Univ. Press, 1962), 180.

37. Willis Fletcher Johnson, *George Harvey* (Boston: Houghton Mifflin, 1929), 80–81. Paragraphs four, five, and six are from the MS in the Berg Collection, NYPL.

38. *Ibid.*, 81.

39. 4 Nov. 1904, *Mark Twain's Letters* (New York: Harper, 1917), II, 762–63.

40. *Ibid.*, 766–67.

41. *MTA*, II, 190.

42. *Ibid.*, 199.

43. Fatout, 591.

44. *MTHL*, I, 37–40.

45. *MTE*, 1–4.

46. *Ibid.*, 12 Sept. 1908, p. 34.

47. MS #85, A1911, MTP.

48. Stefan Lorant, *The Life and Times of Theodore Roosevelt* (Garden City, N.Y.: Doubleday, 1959), 556.

49. NAR, CLXXX (March 1905).

50. " 'Russian Liberty Has Had Its Last Chance,' says Mark Twain," *Boston Globe* (29 Aug. 1905).

51. 30 March 1906, *MTA*, II, 292–93.

52. SLC to TR, 28 Nov. 1905, ALS in MTP; the MS has been labeled "Copy" in another hand, but it may have been a draft since it embodies corrections; and it may never have been sent.

53. 28 Nov. 1905, ALS in MTP; Pringle, 245.

54. 11 Dec. 1905, to Mr. Twe, ALS in MTP; and 26 Dec. 1905, to T.B. Aldrich, ALS in MTP.

55. SLC to Dr. Thomas Barbour, Secretary of the Congo Reform Association, 8 Jan. 1906, AL unfinished and unsigned, in MTP.

56. 8 Jan. 1906, to Dr. Thomas Barbour, TLS in MTP.

57. 10 Feb. 1906, to Dr. Thomas Barbour, copy in MTP.

58. Hunt Hawkins, "Mark Twain's Involvement with the Congo Reform Movement: 'A Fury of Generous Indignation,' " *New England Quarterly*, LI (June 1978), 173.

59. *Ibid.*, 173–74.

60. Fatout, 513–14; Justin Kaplan, *Mr. Clemens and Mark Twain* (New York: Simon and Schuster, 1966), 367–68.

61. Pringle, 474, quoting TR to John E. Lodge, 23 April 1906.

62. 18 Oct. 1907, *MTE*, 8–9.

63. 14 July 1908, *MTE*, 30–31.

64. *Washington Herald*, 6 Dec. 1906, in Louis J. Budd, ed., *Interviews with Samuel L. Clemens, American Literary Realism*, X (Winter 1977), 79. See also Harbaugh, 303–308. The soldiers included six Medal of Honor winners.

65. 14 July 1908, *MTE*, 31–32.

66. *New York Times*, 6 June 1973; 5 Aug. 1973; 11 Jan. 1974.

67. *MTHL*, 23 Oct. 1898, II, 680.

Notes

CHAPTER 4

1. Elmer Ellis, *Mr. Dooley's America, A Life of Finley Peter Dunne* (New York: Knopf, 1941), 251. Hereafter Ellis.
2. *Ibid.*, 305.
3. 7 Jan. 1907, FPD to TR, *Theodore Roosevelt Papers*, P73–4739.
4. F.P. Dunne, *Mr. Dooley in the Hearts of his Countrymen* (Boston: Small, Maynard, 1899), 15. Hereafter *Hearts*.
5. Ellis, 111.
6. "Certain of the Chicago School of Fiction," *NAR*, CLXXVI (May 1903), 746.
7. *Hearts*, 22.
8. Ellis, 307.
9. *Mr. Dooley Remembers, the Informal Memoirs of Finley Peter Dunne*, Philip Dunne, ed. (Boston: Little, Brown, 1963), 185. Hereafter *Mr. Dooley Remembers*.
10. *Harper's Weekly*, XLIII (25 Nov. 1899), 1195, rpt. in F.P. Dunne, *Mr. Dooley's Philosophy* (New York: R.H. Russell, 1900), 13, 14, 15, 18. Hereafter *Mr. Dooley's Philosophy*.
11. 28 Nov. 1899, *Letters TR*, II, 1099.
12. 16 Jan. 1900, *Letters TR*, II, 1134.
13. *Mr. Dooley Remembers*, 186.
14. 14 Dec. 1899, to H.C. Lodge, *Letters TR*, II, 1110.
15. *Mr. Dooley Remembers*, 187–89; Pringle, 220–23.
16. TR to FPD, 24 June 1901, *Theodore Roosevelt Papers*, P73–5094, and FPD to TR, 2 July 1901, P73–4684.
17. FPD to TR, 14 Sept. 1901, *Theodore Roosevelt Papers* P73–4686; TR to FPD, 11 Nov. 1901, *Letters TR*, III, 195; FPD to TR, 12 Nov. 1901, *Theodore Roosevelt Papers*, P73–4690.
18. FPD to TR, 8 Dec. 1902, *Theodore Roosevelt Papers*, P73–4699; TR to FPD, 10 Dec. 1902.
19. F.P. Dunne, *Observations of Mr. Dooley* (New York: Harper, 1902), 223–28. Hereafter *Observations*.
20. TR to FPD, 6 April 1904, P73–4711; FPD to TR, 23 Dec. 1904, P73–4719, *Theodore Roosevelt Papers*; F.P. Dunne, *Dissertations by Mr. Dooley* (New York: Harper, 1906), 213–18, hereafter *Dissertations*; and TR to FPD, 23 Nov. 1904, *Letters TR*, IV, 1040–43; FPD to TR, 28 Dec. 1905, *Theodore Roosevelt Papers*, P73–4730; TR to FPD, 18 June 1906, P73–4730; FPD to TR, 6 July 1906, P73–4730.
21. FPD to TR, 7 Jan. 1907, *Theodore Roosevelt Papers*, P73–4739.
22. "In the Interpreter's House," *American Magazine*, LXVII (March 1909), 527–30.
23. "Mr. Dooley: On Colonel Roosevelt's Western Tour," *Harper's Weekly*, XLIV (13 Oct. 1900), 973.
24. *Ibid.*, 74.
25. 22 Nov. 1900, *Theodore Roosevelt Papers*, P73–5092.

26. *Mr. Dooley's Philosophy*, 229–33.
27. "Bad Men from the West," *Observations*, 98, 99, 102, 103.
28. Pringle, 354.
29. Herman Hagedorn, *The Roosevelt Family of Sagamore Hill* (New York: Macmillan, 1954), 212, quoting unidentified source.
30. Lorant, *Theodore Roosevelt*, 567.
31. Ellis, 248.
32. F.P. Dunne, *Mr. Dooley in Peace and War* (Boston: Small, Maynard, 1899), 54–55. Hereafter *Peace and War*.
33. *Hearts*, 15–17.
34. *Dissertations*, 213–18.
35. *Letters TR*, IV, 1040–42.
36. 1 Dec. 1904, *Theodore Roosevelt Papers*, P73–4718.
37. Ellis, 173–74.
38. *Ibid.*, 175–76, quoted from the *New York Journal*, 12 Oct. 1902.
39. TR to FPD, Oct. 1902, in Mark Sullivan, *Our Times* (New York: Scribner's, 1927), II, 443.
40. 23 Oct. 1902, P73–4698, *Theodore Roosevelt Papers;* Pringle, 264–78; Harbaugh, 166–181.
41. *Mr. Dooley Remembers*, 200–201; Pringle, 440–45.
42. Mark Sullivan, *Our Times*, II, 411.
43. "Immigration," *Observations*, 49.
44. *Dissertations*, 249, 254; Harbaugh, 257–60.
45. *Ibid.*, 64.
46. Pringle, 430; *Works TR*, XV, 270–409.
47. *Observations*, 49, 50, 52.
48. Ellis, 117.
49. *Mr. Dooley's Philosophy*, 49–53.
50. *Ibid.*, 78.
51. 16 Jan. 1900, *Letters TR*, II, 1134.
52. Pringle, 248–49.
53. F.P. Dunne, *Mr. Dooley's Opinions* (New York: Harper, 1901), 207–12. Hereafter *Opinions*.
54. *Dissertations*, 185–90.
55. *Ibid.*, 187.
56. *Ibid.*, 190.
57. Pringle, "The Japanese Menace," Bk. 2, Ch. X.
58. F.P. Dunne, *Mr. Dooley Says* (New York: Scribner's, 1910), 195. Hereafter *Mr. Dooley Says*.
59. *Works TR*, XII, 184; Pringle, 470–72.
60. *Dissertations*, 141.
61. *Ibid.*, 221–23, 225.
62. *Works TR*, XIII, 319–610; XX, 30–56.
63. *Harper's Weekly*, XLIV (13 Oct. 1900), 973–74.
64. *Opinions*, 125–29.
65. *Ibid.*, 181.

66. *Observations*, 186–87.
67. Pringle, 446–49.
68. *Observations*, 59–61.
69. *Mr. Dooley's Philosophy*, 262; *Works TR*, XIII, "Co-operation and the Simple Life," 530–35; *Dissertations*, 229–34.
70. Ellis, 171.
71. *Ibid.*, 118.
72. *Hearts*, 6; *Chicago Journal*, 18 March 1899, as quoted in Charles Fanning, *Finley Peter Dunne and Mr. Dooley, the Chicago Years* (Lexington: Univ. Press of Kentucky, 1978), 200.
73. "Mr. Dooley: On Colonel Roosevelt's Western Tour," *Harper's Weekly*, XLIV (13 Oct. 1900), 974.
74. "Mr. Wu," *Mr. Dooley's Philosophy*, 88.
75. "The Future of China," *Mr. Dooley's Philosophy*, 94.
76. *Opinions*, 26.
77. *Observations*, 115–20.
78. *Ibid.*, 91–94.
79. *Ibid.* 123–29.
80. *Dissertations*, 207–10.
81. See "A Broken Friendship," *Mr. Dooley Says*, 102, 108.
82. *Mr. Dooley Remembers*, 210.
83. *NAR*, CLXXVI (May 1903), 745.
84. *Mr. Dooley Says*, 129–31; Ellis, 281.

SELECTED BIBLIOGRAPHY

I have read and profited from Clyde Dornbusch's unpublished doctoral dissertation, completed at Duke University in 1957, "Theodore Roosevelt's Literary Taste and Relationship with Authors," an excellent survey of a broad subject. My focus differs distinctly from Dornbusch's, however, in that I take the angle of vision of Howells, Clemens, and Dunne and present what they saw in greater breadth and depth and detail. Ellen Moers has written a bright, concentrated essay on TR and New York City writers, "Theodore Roosevelt: Literary Feller," in *Columbia University Forum*, Summer 1963 (VI, 10–16).

Brooks, Van Wyck. *Howells, His Life and World*. New York: Dutton, 1959.
Budd, Louis J. *Mark Twain, Social Philosopher*. Bloomington: Indiana Univ. Press, 1962.
Dunne, Finley Peter. *Dissertations by Mr. Dooley*. New York: Harper, 1906.
———. *Mr. Dooley in Peace and War*. Boston: Small, Maynard, 1899.
———. *Mr. Dooley in the Hearts of His Countrymen*. Boston: Small, Maynard, 1899.
———. *Mr. Dooley Remembers, The Informal Memoirs of Finley Peter Dunne*, ed. Philip Dunne. Boston: Little, Brown, 1963.
———. *Mr. Dooley Says*. New York: Scribner's, 1910.
———. *Mr. Dooley's Opinions*. New York: Harper, 1901.
———. *Mr. Dooley's Philosophy*. New York: R.H. Russell, 1900.
———. *Observations of Mr. Dooley*. New York: Harper, 1902.
Edel, Leon. *Henry James the Master: 1901–1916*. Philadelphia: Lippincott, 1972.
Ellis, Elmer. *Mr. Dooley's America, A Life of Finley Peter Dunne*. New York: Knopf, 1941.
Fables of Man, ed. John S. Tuckey. Berkeley: Univ. of California Press, 1972.
Fanning, Charles. *Finley Peter Dunne and Mr. Dooley, The Chicago Years*. Lexington: Univ. Press of Kentucky, 1978.
Garland, Hamlin. *Roadside Meetings*. New York: Macmillan, 1930.
Gibson, William M. *The Art of Mark Twain*. New York: Oxford Univ. Press, 1976.

Glasgow, Ellen. *The Woman Within*. New York: Harcourt, Brace, 1954.
Hagedorn, Herman. *The Roosevelt Family of Sagamore Hill*. New York: Macmillan, 1954.
Harbaugh, William Howard. *Power and Responsibility. The Life and Times of Theodore Roosevelt*. New York: Farrar, 1961.
Hill, Hamlin. *Mark Twain, God's Fool*. New York: Harper, 1973.
Howells, William Dean. *The Life in Letters of William Dean Howells*, ed. Mildred Howells. 2 vols. New York: Doubleday, 1928.
Johnson, Willis Fletcher. *George Harvey*. Boston: Houghton Mifflin, 1929.
Lewis, R.W.B. *Edith Wharton: A Biography*. New York: Harper, 1975.
Lorant, Stefan. *The Life and Times of Theodore Roosevelt*. Garden City, N.Y.: Doubleday, 1959.
Mark Twain-Howells Letters, ed., Henry Nash Smith and William M. Gibson. 2 vols. Cambridge: Harvard Univ. Press, 1960.
Masters, Edgar Lee. *Across Spoon River*. New York: Farrar, 1936.
Mencken, H.L. *The New Mencken Letters*, ed. Carl Bode. New York: Dial, 1977.
————. *Prejudices Second Series*. New York: Knopf, 1920.
Neff, Emery. *Edward Arlington Robinson*. New York: Sloane, 1948.
Pringle, Henry F. *Theodore Roosevelt, A Biography*. New York: Harcourt, Brace, 1931.
Roosevelt as the Poets Saw Him, ed. C.H. Towne. New York: Scribner's, 1923.
Roosevelt, Theodore. *The Letters of Theodore Roosevelt*, ed. Elting E. Morison. 8 vols. Cambridge: Harvard Univ. Press, 1951.
————. *Theodore Roosevelt Papers*. Microfilm.
————. *The Works of Theodore Roosevelt*, ed. Herman Hagedorn. 20 vols., The National Edition. New York: Scribner's, 1926.
Stallman, R.W. *Stephen Crane, A Biography*. New York: Braziller, 1968.
Sullivan, Mark. *Our Times*. New York: Scribner's, 1927.
Twain, Mark. *Mark Twain in Eruption*, ed. Bernard De Voto. New York: Harper, 1940.
————. *Mark Twain Speaking*, ed. Paul Fatout. Iowa City: Univ. of Iowa Press, 1976.
————. *Mark Twain's Autobiography*, ed. A.B. Paine. 2 vols. New York: Harper, 1924.
Wharton, Edith. *A Backward Glance*. New York: Appleton-Century, 1936.

SERIALS BIBLIOGRAPHY

American Literary Realism, X (Winter 1977).
American Magazine, LXVII (March 1909).
Boston Globe (29 Aug. 1905).
Boston Herald (10 June 1907).

Harper's Monthly Magazine, LXXVII (July 1888)–CXIII (Sept. 1906).
Harper's Weekly, XLIII (Nov. 1899)–Supplement (Dec. 1905).
Nation, LXXI (Nov. 1900).
New York Journal (12 Oct. 1902).
New York Sun (26 June 1907).
New York Times (6 June 1973, 5 Aug. 1973, 11 Jan. 1974).
North American Review, CLXXIV (May 1902)–CLXXX (March 1905).
Washington Herald (6 Dec. 1906).

INDEX

Index

The Hodges Lectures

THE BETTER ENGLISH FUND was established in 1947 by John C. Hodges, Professor of English, The University of Tennessee, 1921–1962, and head of the English Department, 1941–1962, on the returns from the *Harbrace College Handbook*, of which he was the author. Over the years, it has been used to support the improvement of teaching and research in the English Department. The Hodges Lectures, inaugurated with the present series, are intended to commemorate this wise and generous bequest.

THE HODGES LECTURES book series is set in ten-point Sabon type with two-point spacing between the lines. Sabon is also used for display. The series format was designed by Jim Billingsley. This title in the series was composed by Williams of Chattanooga, Tennessee, printed by Thomson-Shore, Inc., Dexter, Michigan, and bound by John H. Dekker & Sons, Grand Rapids, Michigan. The paper on which the book is printed bears the watermark of S.D. Warren and is designed for an effective life of at least 300 years.

THE UNIVERSITY OF TENNESSEE PRESS : KNOXVILLE